TOP TEN
THEOLOGIANS

Timothy G. Kimberley

Credo House

TOP TEN THEOLOGIANS READER
© 2013 by Timothy G. Kimberley
All rights reserved.

ISBN: 061578786X
EAN-13: 978-0615787862

Printed in the United States of America.

Dedicated to my beloved children:

Hannah, Silas and Grace

I hope in these pages you'll one day
meet some of daddy's friends and
they'll become your friends too.

TABLE OF CONTENTS

10

TOP TEN

THEOLOGIANS

INTRODUCTION TO THE READER

TOP TEN THEOLOGIANS

This book is a companion to the book *Top Ten Theologians*. In that book you gain insight into the world, life, thoughts, foibles and influence of some of the greatest Christian thinkers to ever live.

In this book you get a taste for the original writings of the people you hopefully came to appreciate in the first book.

It can be a daunting task to pick up and read men like Barth, Edwards, Calvin, Luther and Aquinas. Many people sit down to read their mighty works without much training. You would never try to run a marathon without first becoming comfortable running a mile.

In this volume I ask you to simply run a mile with the greats; giving you the training to one day run a marathon with them.

===== READER =====

WARNING:
THE FOLLOWING PAGES
CONTAIN SOME OF THE DEEPEST
WRITING ON THE PLANET

HEART AND MIND
MAY BE BLOWN

PROCEED WITH
CAUTION

===== TOP TEN THEOLOGIANS =====

IRENAEUS:AGAINST HERESIES EXCERPT WRITTEN 180AD

TOP TEN THEOLOGIANS

BOOK I

PREFACE.

1. INASMUCH(1) as certain men have set the truth aside, and bring in lying words and vain genealogies, which, as the apostle says,(2) "minister questions rather than godly edifying which is in faith," and by means of their craftily-constructed plausibilities draw away the minds of the inexperienced and take them captive, [I have felt constrained, my dear friend, to compose the following treatise in order to expose and counteract their machinations.] These men falsify the oracles of God, and prove themselves evil interpreters of the good word of revelation. They also overthrow the faith of many, by drawing them away, under a pretence of [superior] knowledge, from Him who rounded and adorned the universe; as if, forsooth, they had something more excellent and sublime to reveal, than that God who created the heaven and the earth, and all things that are therein. By means of specious and plausible words, they cunningly allure the simple-minded to inquire into their system; but they nevertheless clumsily destroy them, while they initiate them into their blasphemous and impious

opinions respecting the Demiurge;(3) and these simple ones are unable, even in such a matter, to distinguish falsehood from truth.

2. Error, indeed, is never set forth in its naked deformity, lest, being thus exposed, it should at once be detected. But it is craftily decked out in an attractive dress, so as, by its outward form, to make it appear to the inexperienced (ridiculous as the expression may seem) more true than the truth itself. One(4) far superior to me has well said, in reference to this point, "A clever imitation in glass casts contempt, as it were, on that precious jewel the emerald (which is most highly esteemed by some), unless it come under the eye of one able to test and expose the counterfeit. Or, again, what inexperienced person can with ease detect the presence of brass when it has been mixed up with silver?" Lest, therefore, through my neglect, some should be carried off, even as sheep are by wolves, while they perceive not the true character of these men,-because they outwardly are covered with sheep's clothing (against whom the Lord has enjoined(5) us to be on our guard), and because their language resembles ours, while their sentiments are very different,--I have deemed it my duty (after reading some of the Commentaries, as they call them, of the disciples of Valentinus, and after making myself acquainted with their tenets through personal intercourse with some of them) to unfold to thee, my friend, these portentous and profound mysteries, which do not fall within the range of every intellect, because all have not sufficiently purged(6) their brains. I do this, in order that thou, obtaining an acquaintance with these things, mayest in turn explain them to all those with whom thou art connected, and exhort them to avoid such an abyss of madness and of blasphemy against Christ. I intend, then, to the best of my ability, with brevity and clearness to set forth the opinions of those who are now promulgating heresy. I refer especially to the disciples of Ptolemaeus, whose school may be described as a bud from that of Valentinus. I shall also endeavour, according to my moderate ability, to furnish the means of overthrowing them, by showing how absurd and inconsistent with the truth are their statements. Not that I am practised either in composition or eloquence; but my feeling of affection prompts me to make known to thee and all thy companions those doctrines which have been kept in concealment until now, but which are at last, through the goodness of God, brought to light. "For there is nothing hidden which

shall not be revealed, nor secret that shall not be made known."(1)

3. Thou wilt not expect from me, who am resident among the Keltae,(2) and am accustomed for the most part to use a barbarous dialect, any display of rhetoric, which I have never learned, or any excellence of composition, which I have never practised, or any beauty and persuasiveness of style, to which I make no pretensions. But thou wilt accept in a kindly spirit what I in a like spirit write to thee simply, truthfully, and in my own homely way; whilst thou thyself (as being more capable than I am) wilt expand those ideas of which I send thee, as it were, only the seminal principles; and in the comprehensiveness of thy understanding, wilt develop to their full extent the points on which I briefly touch, so as to set with power before thy companions those things which I have uttered in weakness. In fine, as I (to gratify thy long-cherished desire for information regarding the tenets of these persons) have spared no pains, not only to make these doctrines known to thee, but also to furnish the means of showing their falsity; so shalt thou, according to the grace given to thee by the Lord, prove an earnest and efficient minister to others, that men may no longer be drawn away by the plausible system of these heretics, which I now proceed to describe.(3)

CHAP. I.--ABSURD IDEAS OF THE DISCIPLES OF VALENTINUS AS TO THE ORIGIN, NAME, ORDER, AND CONJUGAL PRODUCTIONS OF THEIR FANCIED AEONS, WITH THE PASSAGES OF SCRIPTURE WHICH THEY ADAPT TO THEIR OPINIONS.

1. THEY maintain, then, that in the invisible and ineffable heights above there exists a certain perfect, pre-existent AEon,(4) whom they call Proarche, Propator, and Bythus, and describe as being invisible and incomprehensible. Eternal and unbegotten, he remained throughout innumerable cycles of ages in profound serenity and quiescence. There existed along with him Ennoea, whom they also call Charis and Sige.(5) At last this Bythus determined to send forth from himself the beginning of all things, and deposited this production (which he had resolved to bring forth) in his contemporary Sige, even as seed is deposited in the womb. She then, having received this seed, and becoming pregnant, gave birth to Nous, who

was both similar and equal to him who had produced him, and was alone capable of comprehending his father's greatness. This Nous they call also Monogenes, and Father, and the Beginning of all Things. Along with him was also produced Aletheia; and these four constituted the first and first-begotten Pythagorean Tetrad, which they also denominate the root of all things. For there are first Bythus and Sige, and then Nous and Aletheia. And Monogenes, perceiving for what purpose he had been produced, also himself sent forth Logos and Zoe, being the father of all those who were to come after him, and the beginning and fashioning of the entire Pleroma. By the conjunction of Logos and Zoo were brought forth Anthropos and Ecclesia; and thus was formed the first-begotten Ogdoad, the root and substance of all things, called among them by four names, viz., Bythus, and Nous, and Logos, and Anthropos. For each of these is masculo-feminine, as follows: Propator was united by a conjunction with his Ennoea; then Monogenes, that is Nous, with Aletheia; Logos with Zoe, and Anthropos with Ecclesia.

2. These AEons having been produced for the glory of the Father, and wishing, by their own efforts, to effect this object, sent forth emanations by means of conjunction. Logos and Zoe, after producing Anthropos and Ecclesia, sent forth other ten AEons, whose names are the following: Bythius and Mixis, Ageratos and Henosis, Autophyes and Hedone, Acinetos and Syncrasis, Monogenes and Macaria.(6) These are the ten AEons whom they declare to have been produced by Logos and Zoe. They then add that Anthropos himself, along with Ecclesia, produced twelve AEons, to whom they give the following names: Paracletus and Pistis, Patricos and Elpis, Metricos and Agape, Ainos and Synesis, Ecclesiasticus and Macariotes, Theletos and Sophia.

3. Such are the thirty AEons in the erroneous system of these men; and they are described as being wrapped up, so to speak, in silence, and known to none [except these professing teachers]. Moreover, they declare that this invisible and spiritual Pleroma of theirs is tripartite, being divided into an Ogdoad, a Decad, and a Duodecad. And for this reason they affirm it was that the "Saviour"--for they do not please to call Him "Lord"--did no work in public during the space of thirty years,(1) thus setting forth

the mystery of these AEons. They maintain also, that these thirty AEons are most plainly indicated in the parable(2) of the labourers sent into the vineyard. For some are sent about the first hour, others about the third hour, others about the sixth hour, others about the ninth hour, and others about the eleventh hour. Now, if we add up the numbers of the hours here mentioned, the sum total will be thirty: for one, three, six, nine, and eleven, when added together, form thirty. And by the hours, they hold that the AEons were pointed out; while they maintain that these are great, and wonderful, and hitherto unspeakable mysteries which it is their special function to develop; and so they proceed when they find anything in the multitude(3) of things contained in the Scriptures which they can adopt and accommodate to their baseless speculations.

CHAP. II.--THE PROPATOR WAS KNOWN TO MONO-GENES ALONE. AMBITION, DISTURBANCE, AND DANGER INTO WHICH SOPHIA FELL; HER SHAPELESS OFFSPRING: SHE IS RESTORED BY HOROS. THE PRODUCTION OF CHRIST AND OF THE HOLY SPIRIT, IN ORDER TO THE COMPLETION OF THE AEONS. MANNER OF THE PRODUCTION OF JESUS.

1. They proceed to tell us that the Propator of their scheme was known only to Monogenes, who sprang from him; in other words, only to Nous, while to all the others he was invisible and incomprehensible. And, according to them, Nous alone took pleasure in contemplating the Father, and exulting in considering his immeasurable greatness; while he also meditated how he might communicate to the rest of the AEons the greatness of the Father, revealing to them how vast and mighty he was, and how he was without beginning,--beyond comprehension, and altogether incapable of being seen. But, in accordance with the will of the Father, Sige restrained him, because it was his design to lead them all to an acquaintance with the aforesaid Propator, and to create within them a desire of investigating his nature. In like manner, the rest of the AEons also, in a kind of quiet way, had a wish to behold the Author of their being, and to contemplate that First Cause which had no beginning.

2. But there rushed forth in advance of the rest that AEon who was much

the latest of them, and was the youngest of the Duodecad which sprang
from Anthropos and Ecclesia, namely Sophia, and suffered passion apart
from the embrace of her consort Theletos. This passion, indeed, first arose
among those who were connected with Nous and Aletheia, but passed as
by contagion to this degenerate Æon, who acted under a pretence of love,
but was in reality influenced by temerity, because she had not, like Nous, enjoyed communion with the perfect Father. This passion, they say, consisted
in a desire to search into the nature of the Father; for she wished, according
to them, to comprehend his greatness. When she could not attain her end,
inasmuch as she aimed at an impossibility, and thus became involved in an
extreme agony of mind, while both on account of the vast profundity as
well as the unsearchable nature of the Father, and on account of the love
she bore him, she was ever stretching herself forward, there was danger lest
she should at last have been absorbed by his sweetness, and resolved into
his absolute essence, unless she had met with that Power which supports
all things, and preserves them outside of the unspeakable greatness. This
power they term Horos; by whom, they say, she was restrained and supported; and that then, having with difficulty been brought back to herself,
she was convinced that the Father is incomprehensible, and so laid aside her
original design, along with that passion which had arisen within her from
the overwhelming influence of her admiration.

3. But others of them fabulously describe the passion and restoration of
Sophia as follows: They say that she, having engaged in an impossible and
impracticable attempt, brought forth an amorphous substance, such as her
female nature enabled her to produce.(4) When she looked upon it, her first
feeling was one of grief, on account of the imperfection of its generation,
and then of fear lest this should end(5) her own existence. Next she lost,
as it were, all command of herself, and was in the greatest perplexity while
endeavouring to discover the cause of all this, and in what way she might
conceal what had happened. Being greatly harassed by these passions, she
at last changed her mind, and endeavoured to return anew to the Father.
When, however, she in some measure made the attempt, strength failed her,
and she became a suppliant of the Father. The other Æons, Nous in particular, presented their supplications along with her. And hence they declare

material substance(1) had its beginning from ignorance and grief, and fear and bewilderment.

4. The Father afterwards produces, in his own image, by means of Monogenes, the above-mentioned Horos, without conjunction,(2) masculo-feminine. For they maintain that sometimes the Father acts in conjunction with Sige, but that at other times he shows himself independent both of male and female. They term this Horos both Stauros and Lytrotes, and Carpistes, and Horothetes, and Metagoges.(3) And by this Horos they declare that Sophia was purified and established, while she was also restored to her proper conjunction. For her enthymesis (or inborn idea) having been taken away from her, along with its supervening passion, she herself certainly remained within the Pleroma; but her enthymesis, with its passion, was separated from her by Horos, fenced(4) off, and expelled from that circle. This enthymesis was, no doubt, a spiritual substance, possessing some of the natural tendencies of an AEon, but at the same time shapeless and without form, because it had received nothing.(5) And on this account they say that it was an imbecile and feminine production.(6)

5. After this substance had been placed outside of the Pleroma of the AEons, and its mother restored to her proper conjunction, they tell us that Monogenes, acting in accordance with the prudent forethought of the Father, gave origin to another conjugal pair, namely Christ and the Holy Spirit (lest any of the AEons should fall into a calamity similar to that of Sophia), for the purpose of fortifying and strengthening the Pleroma, and who at the same time completed the number of the AEons. Christ then instructed them as to the nature of their conjunction, and taught them that those who possessed a comprehension of the Unbegotten were sufficient for themselves.(7) He also announced among them what related to the knowledge of the Father,--namely, that he cannot be understood or comprehended, nor so much as seen or heard, except in so far as he is known by Monogenes only. And the reason why the rest of the AEons possess perpetual existence is found in that part of the Father's nature which is incomprehensible; but the reason of their origin and formation was situated in that which may be comprehended regarding him, that is, in the Son.(8) Christ,

then, who had just been produced, effected these things among them.

6. But the Holy Spirit(9) taught them to give thanks on being all rendered equal among themselves, and led them to a state of true repose. Thus, then, they tell us that the AEons were constituted equal to each other in form and sentiment, so that all became as Nous, and Logos, and Anthropos, and Christus. The female AEons, too, became all as Aletheia, and Zoe, and Spiritus, and Ecclesia. Everything, then, being thus established, and brought into a state of perfect rest, they next tell us that these beings sang praises with great joy to the Propator, who himself shared in the abounding exaltation. Then, out of gratitude for the great benefit which had been conferred on them, the whole Pleroma of the AEons, with one design and desire, and with the concurrence of Christ and the Holy Spirit, their Father also setting the seal of His approval on their conduct, brought together whatever each one had in himself of the greatest beauty and preciousness; and uniting all these contributions so as skilfully to blend the whole, they produced, to the honour and glory of Bythus, a being of most perfect beauty, the very star of the Pleroma, and the perfect fruit [of it], namely Jesus. Him they also speak of under the name of Saviour, and Christ, and patronymically, Logos, and Everything, because He was formed from the contributions of all. And then we are told that, by way of honour, angels of the same nature as Himself were simultaneously produced, to act as His body-guard.

CHAP. III.--TEXTS OF HOLY SCRIPTURE USED BY THESE HERETICS TO SUPPORT THEIR OPINIONS.

1. Such, then, is the account they give of what took place within the Pleroma; such the calamities that flowed from the passion which seized upon the AEon who has been named, and who was within a little of perishing by being absorbed in the universal substance, through her inquisitive searching after the Father; such the consolidation(1) [of that AEon] from her condition of agony by Horos, and Stauros, and Lytrotes, and Carpistes, and Horothetes, and Metagoges.(2) Such also is the account of the generation of the later AEons, namely of the first Christ and of the Holy Spirit, both of whom were produced by the Father after the repentance(3) [of Sophia],

and of the second(4) Christ (whom they also style Saviour), who owed his being to the joint contributions [of the AEons]. They tell us, however, that this knowledge has not been openly divulged, because all are not capable of receiving it, but has been mystically revealed by the Saviour through means of parables to those qualified for understanding it. This has been done as follows. The thirty AEons are indicated (as we have already remarked) by the thirty years during which they say the Saviour performed no public act, and by the parable of the labourers in the vineyard. Paul also, they affirm, very clearly and frequently names these AEons, and even goes so far as to preserve their order, when he says, "To all the generations of the AEons of the AEon."(5) Nay, we ourselves, when at the giving of thanks we pronounce the words, "To AEons of AEons" (for ever and ever), do set forth these AEons. And, in fine, wherever the words AEon or AEons occur, they at once refer them to these beings.

2. The production, again, of the Duodecad of the AEons, is indicated by the fact that the Lord was twelve(7) years of age when He disputed with the teachers of the law, and by the election of the apostles, for of these there were twelve.(8) The other eighteen AEons are made manifest in this way: that the Lord, [according to them,] conversed with His disciples for eighteen months(9) after His resurrection from the dead. They also affirm that these eighteen AEons are strikingly indicated by the first two letters of His name [Ihsous], namely Iota(10) and Eta. And, in like manner, they assert that the ten AEons are pointed out by the letter Iota, which begins His name; while, for the same reason, they tell us the Saviour said, "One Iota, or one tittle, shall by no means pass away until all be fulfilled."(11)

3. They further maintain that the passion which took place in the case of the twelfth AEon is pointed at by the apostasy of Judas, who was the twelfth apostle, and also by the fact that Christ suffered in the twelfth month. For their opinion is, that He continued to preach for one year only after His baptism. The same thing is also most clearly indicated by the case of the woman who suffered from an issue of blood. For after she had been thus afflicted during twelve years, she was healed by the advent of the Saviour, when she had touched the border of His garment; and on this account

the Saviour said, "Who touched me?"(12)--teaching his disciples the mystery which had occurred among the AEons, and the healing of that AEon who had been involved in suffering. For she who had been afflicted twelve years represented that power whose essence, as they narrate, was stretching itself forth, and flowing into immensity; and unless she had touched the garment of the Son,(13) that is, Aletheia of the first Tetrad, who is denoted by the hem spoken of, she would have been dissolved into the general essence(14) [of which she participated]. She stopped short, however, and ceased any longer to suffer. For the power that went forth from the Son (and this power they term Horos) healed her, and separated the passion from her.

4. They moreover affirm that the Saviour(15) is shown to be derived from all the AEons, and to be in Himself everything by the following passage: "Every male that openeth the womb."(16) For He, being everything, opened the womb(17) of the enthymesis of the suffering AEon, when it had been expelled from the Pleroma. This they also style the second Ogdoad, of which we shall speak presently. And they state that it was clearly on this account that Paul said, "And He Himself is all things;"(1) and again, "All things are to Him, and of Him are all things;"(2) and further, "In Him dwelleth all the fulness of the Godhead;"(3) and yet again, "All things are gathered together by God in Christ."(4) Thus do they interpret these and any like passages to be found in Scripture.

5. They show, further, that that Horos of theirs, whom they call by a variety of names, has two faculties,--the one of supporting, and the other of separating; and in so far as he supports and sustains, he is Stauros, while in so far as he divides and separates, he is Horos. They then represent the Saviour as having indicated this twofold faculty: first, the sustaining power, when He said, "Whosoever doth not bear his cross (Stauros), and follow after me, cannot be my disciple;"(5) and again, "Taking up the cross follow me;"(6) but the separating power when He said, "I came not to send peace, but a word."(7) They also maintain that John indicated the same thing when he said, "The fan is in His hand, and He will thoroughly purge the floor, and will gather the wheat into His garner; but the chaff He will burn with fire unquenchable."(8) By this declaration He set forth the faculty of Horos.

For that fan they explain to be the cross (Stauros), which consumes, no doubt, all material(9) objects, as fire does chaff, but it purifies all them that are saved, as a fan does wheat. Moreover, they affirm that the Apostle Paul himself made mention of this cross in the following words: "The doctrine of the cross is to them that perish foolishness, but to us who are saved it is the power of God."(10) And again: "God forbid that I should glory in anything(11) save in the cross of Christ, by whom the world is crucified to me, and I unto the world."

6. Such, then, is the account which they all give of their Pleroma, and of the formation(12) of the universe, striving, as they do, to adapt the good words of revelation to their own wicked inventions. And it is not only from the writings of the evangelists and the apostles that they endeavour to derive proofs for their opinions by means of perverse interpretations and deceitful expositions: they deal in the same way with the law and the prophets, which contain many parables and allegories that can frequently be drawn into various senses, according to the kind of exegesis to which they are subjected. And others(13) of them, with great craftiness, adapted such parts of Scripture to their own figments, lead away captive from the truth those who do not retain a stedfast faith in one God, the Father Almighty, and in one Lord Jesus Christ, the Son of God.

CHAP. IV.--ACCOUNT GIVEN BY THE HERETICS OF THE FORMATION OF ACHAMOTH; ORIGIN OF THE VISIBLE WORLD FROM HER DISTURBANCES.

1. The following are the transactions which they narrate as having occurred outside of the Pleroma: The enthymesis of that Sophia who dwells above, which they also term Achamoth,(14) being removed from the Pleroma, together with her passion, they relate to have, as a matter of course, become violently excited in those places of darkness and vacuity [to which she had been banished]. For she was excluded from light(15) and the Pleroma, and was without form or figure, like an untimely birth, because she had received nothing(16) [from a male parent]. But the Christ dwelling on high took pity upon her; and having extended himself through and beyond Stauros,(17) he imparted a figure to her, but merely as respected substance,

and not so as to convey intelligence.(18) Having effected this, he withdrew
his influence, and returned, leaving Achamoth to herself, in order that she,
becoming sensible of her suffering as being severed from the Pleroma,
might be influenced by the desire of better things, while she possessed in
the meantime a kind of odour of immortality left in her by Christ and the
Holy Spirit. Wherefore also she is called by two names--Sophia after her father (for Sophia is spoken of as being her father), and Holy Spirit from that
Spirit who is along with Christ. Having then obtained a form, along with
intelligence, and being immediately deserted by that Logos who had been
invisibly present with her--that is, by Christ--she strained herself to discover
that light which had forsaken her, but could not effect her purpose, inasmuch as she was prevented by Horos. And as Horos thus obstructed her
further progress, he exclaimed, IAO,(1) whence, they say, this name Iao derived its origin. And when she could not pass by Horos on account of that
passion in which she had been involved, and because she alone had been
left without, she then resigned herself to every sort of that manifold and
varied state of passion to which she was subject; and thus she suffered grief
on the one hand because she had not obtained the object of her desire, and
fear on the other hand, lest life itself should fail her, as light had already
done, while, in addition, she was in the greatest perplexity. All these feelings
were associated with ignorance. And this ignorance of hers was not like that
of her mother, the first Sophia, an AEon, due to degeneracy by means of
passion, but to an [innate] opposition [of nature to knowledge].(2) Moreover, another kind of passion fell upon her her (Achamoth), namely, that of
desiring to return to him who gave her life.

2. This collection [of passions] they declare was the substance of the matter from which this world was formed. For from [her desire of] returning
[to him who gave her life], every soul belonging to this world, and that of
the Demiurge(3) himself, derived its origin. All other things owed their
beginning to her terror and sorrow. For from her tears all that is of a liquid
nature was formed; from her smile all that is lucent; and from her grief and
perplexity all the corporeal elements of the world. For at one time, as they
affirm, she would weep and lament on account of being left alone in the
midst of darkness and vacuity; while, at another time, reflecting on the light
which had forsaken her, she would be filled with joy, and laugh; then, again,

she would be struck with terror; or, at other times, would sink into consternation and bewilderment.

3. Now what follows from all this? No light tragedy comes out of it, as the fancy of every man among them pompously explains, one in one way, and another in another, from what kind of passion and from what element being derived its origin. They have good reason, as seems to me, why they should not feel inclined to teach these things to all in public, but only to such as are able to pay a high price for an acquaintance with such profound mysteries. For these doctrines are not at all similar to those of which our Lord said, "Freely ye have received, freely give."(4) They are, on the contrary, abstruse, and portentous, and profound mysteries, to be got at only with great labour by such as are in love with falsehood. For who would not expend lull that he possessed, if only he might learn in return, that from the tears of the enthymesis of the AEon involved in passion, seas, and fountains, and rivers, and every liquid substance derived its origin; that light burst forth from her smile; and that from her perplexity and consternation the corporeal elements of the world had their formation?

4. I feel somewhat inclined myself to contribute a few hints towards the .development of their system. For when I perceive that waters are in part fresh, such as fountains, rivers, showers, and so on, and in part salt; such as those in the sea, I reflect with myself that all such waters cannot be derived from her tears, inasmuch as these are of a saline quality only. It is clear, therefore, that the waters which are salt are alone those which are derived from her tears. But it is probable that she, in her intense agony and perplexity, was covered with perspiration. And hence, following out their notion, we may conceive that fountains and rivers, and all the fresh water in the world, are due to this source. For it is difficult, since we know that all tears are of the same quality, to believe that waters both salt and fresh proceeded from them. The more plausible supposition is, that some are from her tears, and some from her perspiration. And since there are also in the world certain waters which are hot and acrid in their nature, thou must be left to guess their origin, how and whence. Such are some of the results of their hypothesis.

5. They go on to state that, when the mother Achamoth had passed through all sorts of passion, and had with difficulty escaped from them, she turned herself to supplicate the light which had forsaken her, that is, Christ. He, however, having returned to the Pleroma, and being probably unwilling again to descend from it, sent forth to her the Paraclete, that is, the Saviour.(5) This being was endowed with all power by the Father, who placed everything under his authority, the AEons(6) doing so likewise, so that "by him were all things, visible and invisible, created, thrones, divinities, dominions."(7) He then was sent to her along with his contemporary angels. And they related that Achamoth, filled with reverence, at first veiled herself through modesty, but that by and by, when she had looked upon him with all his endowments, and had acquired strength from his appearance, she ran forward to meet him. He then imparted to her form as respected intelligence, and brought healing to her passions, separating them from her, but not so as to drive them out of thought altogether. For it was not possible that they should be annihilated as in the former case,(1) because they had already taken root and acquired strength [so as to possess an indestructible existence]. All that he could do was to separate them and set them apart, and then commingle and condense them, so as to transmute them from incorporeal passion into unorganized matter.(2) He then by this process conferred upon them a fitness and a nature to become concretions and corporeal structures, in order that two substances should be formed,--the one evil, resulting from the passions, and the other subject indeed to suffering, but originating from her conversion. And on this account (i.e., on account of this hypostatizing of ideal matter) they say that the Saviour virtually(3) created the world. But when Achamoth was freed from her passion, she gazed with rapture on the dazzling vision of the angels that were with him; and in her ecstasy, conceiving by them, they tell us that she brought forth new beings, partly after her oven image, and partly a spiritual progeny after the image of the Saviour's attendants.

CHAP. V.--FORMATION OF THE DEMIURGE; DESCRIPTION OF HIM. HE IS THE CREATOR OF EVERYTHING OUTSIDE OF THE PLEROMA.

1. These three kinds of existence, then, having, according to them, been

now formed,--one from the passion, which was matter; a second from the conversion, which was animal; and the third, that which she (Achamoth) herself brought forth, which was spiritual,--she next addressed herself to the task of giving these form. But she could not succeed in doing this as respected the spiritual existence, because it was of the same nature with herself. She therefore applied herself to give form to the animal substance which had proceeded from her own conversion, and to bring forth to light the instructions of the Saviour.(4) And they say she first formed out of animal substance him who is Father and King of all things, both of these which are of the same nature with himself, that is, animal substances, which they also call right-handed, and those which sprang from the passion, and from matter, which they call left-handed. For they affirm that he formed all the things which came into existence after him, being secretly impelled thereto by his mother. From this circumstance they style him Metropator,(5) Apator, Demiurge, and Father, saying that he is Father of the substances on the right hand, that is, of the animal, but Demiurge of those on the left, that is, of the material, while he is at the same time the king of all. For they say that this Enthymesis, desirous of making all things to the honour of the AEons, formed images of them, or rather that the Saviour(6) did so through her instrumentality. And she, in the image(7) of the invisible Father, kept herself concealed from the Demiurge. But he was in the image of the only-begotten Son, and the angels and archangels created by him were in the image of the rest of the AEons.

2. They affirm, therefore, that he was constituted the Father and God of everything outside of the Pleroma, being the creator of all animal and material substances. For he it was that discriminated these two kinds of existence hitherto confused, and made corporeal from incorporeal substances, fashioned things heavenly and earthly, and became the Framer (Demiurge) of things material and animal, of those on the right and those on the left, of the light and of the heavy, and of those tending upwards as well as of those tending downwards. He created also seven heavens, above which they say that he, the Demiurge, exists. And on this account they term him Hebdomas, and his mother Achamoth Ogdoads, preserving the number of the first-begotten and primary Ogdoad as the Pleroma. They affirm, moreover, that these seven heavens are intelligent, and speak of them as being

angels, while they refer to the Demiurge himself as being an angel bearing a likeness to God; and in the same strain, they declare that Paradise, situated above the third heaven, is a fourth angel possessed of power, from whom Adam derived certain qualities while he conversed with him.

3. They go on to say that the Demiurge imagined that he created all these things of himself, while he in reality made them in conjunction with the productive power of Achamoth. He formed the heavens, yet was ignorant of the heavens; he fashioned man, yet knew not man; he brought to light the earth, yet had no acquaintance with the earth; and, in like manner. they declare that he was ignorant of the forms of all that he made, and knew not even of the existence of his own mother, but imagined that he himself was all things. They further affirm that his mother originated this opinion in his mind, because she desired to bring him forth possessed of such a character that he should be the head and source of his own essence, and the absolute ruler over every kind of operation [that was afterwards attempted]. This mother they also call Ogdoad, Sophia; Terra, Jerusalem, Holy Spirit, and, with a masculine reference, Lord.(1) Her place of habitation is an intermediate one, above the Demiurge indeed, but below and outside of the Pleroma, even to the end.(2)

4. As, then, they represent all material substance to be formed from three passions, viz., fear, grief, and perplexity, the account they give is as follows: Animal substances originated from fear and from conversion; the Demiurge they also describe as owing his origin to conversion; but the existence of all the other animal substances they ascribe to fear, such as the souls of irrational animals, and of wild beasts, and men. And on this account, he (the Demiurge), being incapable of recognising any spiritual essences, imagined himself to be God alone, and declared through the prophets, "I am God, and besides me there is none else."(3) They further teach that the spirits of wickedness derived their origin from grief. Hence the devil, whom they also call Cosmocrator (the ruler of the world), and the demons, and the angels, and every wicked spiritual being that exists, found the source Of their existence. They represent the Demiurge as being the son of that mother of theirs (Achamoth), and Cosmocrator as the creature of the Demiurge. Cosmocrator has knowledge of what is above himself, because he is a spirit

of wickedness; but the Demiurge is ignorant of such things, inasmuch as he is merely animal. Their mother dwells in that place which is above the heavens, that is, in the intermediate abode; the Demiurge in the heavenly place, that is, in the hebdomad; but the Cosmocrator in this our world. The corporeal elements of the world, again, sprang, as we before remarked, from bewilderment and perplexity, as from a more ignoble source. Thus the earth arose from her state of stupor; water from the agitation caused by her fear; air from the consolidation of her grief; while fire, producing death and corruption, was inherent in all these elements, even as they teach that ignorance also lay concealed in these three passions.

5. Having thus formed the world, he (the Demiurge) also created the earthy [part of] man, not taking him from this dry earth, but from an invisible substance consisting of fusible and fluid matter, and then afterwards, as they define the process, breathed into him the animal part of his nature. It was this latter which was created after his image and likeness. The material part, indeed, was very near to. God, so far as the image went, but not of the same substance with him. The animal, on the Other hand, was so in respect to likeness; and hence his substance was called the spirit of life, because it took its rise from a spiritual outflowing. After all this, he was, they say, enveloped all round with a covering of skin; and by this they mean the outward sensitive flesh.

6. But they further affirm that the Demiurge himself was ignorant of that offspring of his mother Achamoth, which she brought forth as a consequence of her contemplation of those angels who waited on the Saviour, and which was, like herself, of a spiritual nature. She took advantage of this ignorance to deposit it (her production) in him without his knowledge, in order that, being by his instrumentality infused into that animal soul proceeding from himself, and being thus carried as in a womb in this material body, while it gradually increased in strength, might in course of time become fitted for the reception of perfect rationality.(4) Thus it came to pass, then, according to them, that, without any knowledge on the part of the Demiurge, the man formed by his inspiration was at the same time, through an unspeakable providence, rendered a spiritual man by the simultaneous inspiration received from Sophia. For, as he was ignorant of his mother, so

neither did he recognise her offspring. This [offspring] they also declare to be the Ecclesia, an emblem of the Ecclesia which is above. This, then, is the kind of man whom they conceive of: he has his animal soul from the Demiurge, his body from the earth, his fleshy part from matter, and his spiritual man from the mother Achamoth.

KARL BARTH: BARMEN DECLARATION

══════ TOP TEN THEOLOGIANS ══════

Theological Declaration of Barmen

Written by Karl Barth and the confessing church in Nazi Germany in response to Hitler's national church. Its central doctrines concern the sin of idolatry and the lordship of Christ

I. An Appeal to the Evangelical Congregations and Christians in Germany

8.01 The Confessional Synod of the German Evangelical Church met in Barmen, May 29-31, 1934. Here representatives from all the German Confessional Churches met with one accord in a confession of the one Lord of the one, holy, apostolic Church. In fidelity to their Confession of Faith, members of Lutheran, Reformed, and United Churches sought a common message for the need and temptation of the Church in our day. With gratitude to God they are convinced that they have been given a common word to utter. It was not their intention to found a new Church or to form a union. For nothing was farther from their minds than the abolition of the confessional status of our Churches. Their intention was, rather, to withstand in faith and unanimity the destruction of the Confession of Faith, and thus of the Evangelical Church in Germany. In opposition to attempts to establish the unity of the German Evangelical Church by means of false doctrine, by the use of force and insincere practices, the Confessional Synod insists that the unity of the Evangelical Churches in Germany can come only from the Word of God in faith through the Holy Spirit. Thus alone is the Church renewed.

8.02 Therefore the Confessional Synod calls upon the congregations to range themselves behind it in prayer, and steadfastly to gather around those pastors and teachers who are loyal to the Confessions.

8.03 Be not deceived by loose talk, as if we meant to oppose the unity of the German nation! Do not listen to the seducers who pervert our intentions, as if we wanted to break up the unity of the German Evangelical Church or to forsake the Confessions of the Fathers!

8.04 Try the spirits whether they are of God! Prove also the words of the Confessional Synod of the German Evangelical Church to see whether they agree with Holy Scripture and with the Confessions of the Fathers. If you find that we are speaking contrary to Scripture, then do not listen to us! But if you find that we are taking our stand upon Scripture, then let no fear or temptation keep you from treading with us the path of faith and obedience to the Word of God, in order that God's people be of one mind upon earth and that we in faith experience what he himself has said: "I will never leave you, nor forsake you." Therefore, "Fear not, little flock, for it is your Father's good pleasure to give you the kingdom."

II. Theological Declaration Concerning the Present Situation of the German Evangelical Church

8.05 According to the opening words of its constitution of July 11, 1933, the German Evangelical Church is a federation of Confessional Churches that grew our of the Reformation and that enjoy equal rights. The theological basis for the unification of these Churches is laid down in Article 1 and Article 2(1) of the constitution of the German Evangelical Church that was recognized by the Reich Government on July 14, 1933:

> Article 1. The inviolable foundation of the German Evangelical Church is the gospel of Jesus Christ as it is attested for us in Holy Scripture and brought to light again in the Confessions of the Reformation. The full powers that the Church needs for its mission are hereby determined and limited.

> Article 2 (1). The German Evangelical Church is divided into member Churches Landeskirchen).

8.06 We, the representatives of Lutheran, Reformed, and United Churches, of free synods, Church assemblies, and parish organizations united in the Confessional Synod of the German Evangelical Church, declare that we stand together on the ground of the German Evangelical Church as a federation of German Confessional Churches. We are bound together by the confession of the one Lord of the one, holy, catholic, and apostolic Church.

8.07 We publicly declare before all evangelical Churches in Germany that what they hold in common in this Confession is grievously imperiled, and with it the unity of the German Evangelical Church. It is threatened by the teaching methods and actions of the ruling Church party of the "German Christians" and of the Church administration carried on by them. These have become more and more apparent during the first year of the existence of the German Evangelical Church. This threat consists in the fact that the theological basis, in which the German Evangelical Church is united, has been continually and systematically thwarted and rendered ineffective by alien principles, on the part of the leaders and spokesmen of the "German Christians" as well as on the part of the Church administration. When these principles are held to be valid, then, according to all the Confessions in force among us, the Church ceases to be the Church and the German Evangelical Church, as a federation of Confessional Churches, becomes intrinsically impossible.

8.08 As members of Lutheran, Reformed, and United Churches we may and must speak with one voice in this matter today. Precisely because we want to be and to remain faithful to our various Confessions, we may not keep silent, since we believe that we have been given a common message to utter in a time of common need and temptation. We commend to God what this may mean for the interrelations of the Confessional Churches.

8.09 In view of the errors of the "German Christians" of the present Reich Church government which are devastating the Church and also therefore breaking up the unity of the German Evangelical Church, we confess the following evangelical truths:

8.10 - 1. "I am the way, and the truth, and the life; no one comes to the Father, but by me." (John 14.6). "Truly, truly, I say to you, he who does not enter the sheepfold by the door, but climbs in by another way, that man is a thief and a robber. . . . I am the door; if anyone enters by me, he will be saved." (John 10:1, 9.)

8.11 Jesus Christ, as he is attested for us in Holy Scripture, is the one Word of God which we have to hear and which we have to trust and obey in life and in death.

8.12 We reject the false doctrine, as though the church could and would have to acknowledge as a source of its proclamation, apart from and besides this one Word of God, still other events and powers, figures and truths, as God's revelation.

8.13 - 2. "Christ Jesus, whom God has made our wisdom, our righteousness and sanctification and redemption." (1 Cor. 1:30.)

8.14 As Jesus Christ is God's assurance of the forgiveness of all our sins, so, in the same way and with the same seriousness he is also God's mighty claim upon our whole life. Through him befalls us a joyful deliverance from the godless fetters of this world for a free, grateful service to his creatures.

8.15 We reiect the false doctrine, as though there were areas of our life in which we would not belong to Jesus Christ, but to other lords--areas in which we would not need justification and sanctification through him.

8.16 - 3. "Rather, speaking the truth in love, we are to grow up in every way into him who is the head, into Christ, from whom the whole body [is] joined and knit together." (Eph. 4:15,16.)

8.17 The Christian Church is the congregation of the brethren in which Jesus Christ acts presently as the Lord in Word and sacrament through the Holy Spirit. As the Church of pardoned sinners, it has to testify in the midst of a sinful world, with its faith as with its obedience, with its message as with its order, that it is solely his property, and that it lives and wants to live solely from his comfort and from his direction in the expectation of his appearance.

8.18 We reject the false doctrine, as though the Church were permitted to abandon the form of its message and order to its own pleasure or to changes in prevailing ideological and political convictions.

8.19 - 4. "You know that the rulers of the Gentiles lord it over them, and their great men excercise authority over them. It shall not be so among you; but whoever would be great among you must be your srvant." (Matt. 20:25,26.)

8.20 The various offices in the Church do not establish a dominion of some over the others; on the contrary, they are for the excercise of the ministry entrusted to and enjoined upon the whole congregation.

8.21 We reject the false doctrine, as though the Church, apart from this ministry, could and were permitted to give itself, or allow to be given to it, special leaders vested with ruling powers.

8.22 - 5. "Fear God. Honor the emperor." (1 Peter 2:17.)
Scripture tells us that, in the as yet unredeemed world in which the Church

also exists, the State has by divine appointment the task of providing for
justice and peace. [It fulfills this task] by means of the threat and exercise
of force, according to the measure of human judgment and human ability. The Church acknowledges the benefit of this divine appointment in
gratitude and reverence before him. It calls to mind the Kingdom of God,
God's commandment and righteousness, and thereby the responsibility
both of rulers and of the ruled. It trusts and obeys the power of the Word
by which God upholds all things.

8.23 We reject the false doctrine, as though the State, over and beyond its
special commision, should and could become the single and totalitarian
order of human life, thus fulfilling the Church's vocation as well.

8.24 We reject the false doctrine, as though the Church, over and beyond
its special commission, should and could appropriate the characteristics,
the tasks, and the dignity of the State, thus itself becoming an organ of the
State.

8.25 - 6. "Lo, I am with you always, to the close of the age." (Matt. 28:20.)
"The word of God is not fettered." (2 Tim. 2:9.)

8.26 The Church's commission, upon which its freedom is founded, consists in delivering the message of th free grace of God to all people in
Christ's stead, and therefore in the ministry of his own Word and work
through sermon and sacrament.

8.27 We reject the false doctrine, as though the Church in human arrogance
could place the Word and work of the Lord in the service of any arbitrarily
chosen desires, purposes, and plans.

8.28 The Confessional Synod of the German Evangelical Church declares
that it sees in the acknowledgment of these truths and in the rejection of
these errors the indispensable theological basis of the German Evangelical Church as a federation of Confessional Churches. It invites all who are
able to accept its declaration to be mindful of these theological principles in

their decisions in Church politics. It entreats all whom it concerns to return to the unity of faith, love, and hope.

ANSELM: A MEDITATION ON HUMAN REDEMPTION WRITTEN 1099AD

═══════════ TOP TEN THEOLOGIANS ═══════════

0 Christian soul, soul raised up from grievous death, soul re- deemed and freed by the blood of God from wretched bondage: arouse your mind, remember your resurrection, contemplate your redemption and liberation. Consider anew where and what the strength of your salvation is, spend time in meditating upon this strength, delight in reflecting upon it. Shake off your disinclination, constrain yourself, strive with your mind toward this end. Taste the goodness of your Redeemer, be af lame with love for your Savior, chew His words as a honey-comb, suck out their flavor, which is sweeter than honey, swallow their health-giving sweet- ness. Chew by thinking, suck by understanding, swallow by loving and rejoicing. Rejoice in chewing, be glad in sucking, delight in swallowing.

Where, then, and what is the strength and might of your sal- vation? As- suredly, Christ has resurrected you. That Good Samar- itan has healed you, that Good Friend has redeemed and freed you by [sacrificing] His own soul [life]. Yes, it was Christ. Therefore, the strength of Christ is the strength of your salvation. Where is the strength of Christ? Surely horns are in His hands; there His strength is hidden. Horns are indeed in His hands because His hands were nailed to the arms of the cross. But what strength can there be in such great weakness, what sublimity in such great humiliation, what worthy of reverence in such great contempt? But surely because it is [disguised] in weakness it is something hidden, because [veiled] in humiliation it is something concealed, because [covered with] contempt it is something unseen. 0 hidden might! A man appended to a cross suspends the eternal death impend- ing over the human race; a man fastened to a cross unfastens a world affixed to endless death! 0 concealed power! A man con- demned with thieves saves men condemned with demons; a man stretched out on a cross draws all things unto Himself! 0 unseen strength! One soul yielded up in the torment [of crucifixion] draws countless souls [from the torments of] Hell; a man undergoes bodily death and abolishes spiritual death!

Why did you, 0 good Lord, gracious Redeemer, mighty Savior, why did You veil such great strength with such great lowliness? Was it in order to deceive the Devil, who by deceiving man thrust him forth from Paradise? Surely, Truth deceives no one; someone deceives himself if he does not know the truth, if he does not be- lieve it. He deceives himself if, seeing the truth, he hates it or de- spises it; thus, Truth deceives no one. Well, then, [did You con- ceal Your power] in order that the Devil might deceive himself? Surely, just as Truth deceives no one, so it does not intend that anyone deceive himself, (even though we do say that Truth intends this when Truth permits it to occur). For You did not assume a human nature in order to conceal what was known about You but in order to reveal what was unknown about You. You said that You were truly divine and truly human, and You demon- strated this fact through Your works. The hiddenness was unavoidable, not delib- erate. The reason that the event occurred as it did was not in order to be hidden, but in order to be performed in the right way. [It happened in that way] not in order to deceive anyone, but in order to be done as was fitting. If this event is called concealed, then it is called so only because it is not revealed to everyone. Al- though Truth does not manifest itself to everyone, it does not with- hold itself from anyone. Therefore, 0 Lord, in becoming incarnate it was not Your purpose to deceive anyone or to cause anyone to deceive himself. You remained in the truth in every respect so that You might do what had to be done in the way it had to be done. Hence, let anyone who has deceived himself regarding Your truth complain not about You but about the falsehood in himself.

Did the Devil justly have against God or against man some claim which obliged God to act against him on man's behalf in this manner [i.e., by incarnation] before acting by open force, so that when the Devil unjustly killed a just man [Jesus] he would justly lose the power he was holding over unjust men? But surely God did not owe the Devil anything except punishment. Nor did man [owe the Devil anything] except requital, so that just as man by sin- ning permitted himself easily to be defeated by the Devil, so by keeping justice intact even on pain of death, he would defeat the Devil. But even this [conquering of the Devil] man owed only to God; for he sinned against God, not against the Devil. Nor did he belong to the Devil; rather both man and the Devil belonged to God. But even in vexing man the Devil acted not out of zeal for justice but out of zeal for iniquity. God did not command [this vexation]; He [only] permitted it. God's justice, not the Devil's, required [man's punishment]. Therefore, the Devil had no claim which obliged God to conceal His power from him or to postpone its use against him in order to secure man's salvation.

Did some necessity compel the Most High thus to humble Himself as He did; was the Almighty compelled to toil in order to accomplish so great a thing? But all necessity and impossibility are subject to His will. Indeed, what He wills must occur; and what He does not will cannot occur. Therefore, He acted of His own will; and because His will is always good, He acted out of goodness alone. God did not need to secure man's salvation in the way He did; but human nature needed in that way to make satisfaction to God. God did not need to suffer such troubles; but man needed to be reconciled in this way. God did not need thus to humble Himself; but man needed in this way to be rescued from the depth of Hell. The Divine Nature did not need, and was not able, to be abased or to toil. It was necessary for human nature to do all these things in order to be restored to that end for which it was created. But neither human nature nor anyone other than God Himself was able to accomplish these things. Man is not restored to that end for which he was made unless he attains to the likeness of those angels in whom there is no sin. This attainment cannot possibly occur unless the remission of all sins is obtained. And remission occurs only by means of an antecedent complete satisfaction.

This satisfaction ought to be such that the sinner or someone on his behalf gives to God something of his own which is not owed—something which exceeds everything that is not God. For to sin is to dishonor God; and man ought not to dishonor God even if [as a consequence] it were necessary for everything that is other than God to be destroyed. Therefore, without doubt, un- changing truth and clear reason demand that the sinner give to God, in place of the honor stolen, something greater than that for which he ought not to have dishonored God. But human nature by itself did not have this payment. And without the required satisfaction human nature could not be reconciled, lest Divine Justice leave a sin unreckoned-with in His kingdom. Therefore, Divine Goodness gave assistance. The Son of God assumed a human nature into His own person, so that in this person He was the God- man, who possessed what exceeded not only every be- ing which is not God but also every debt which sinners ought to pay. And since He owed nothing for Himself, He paid this sum for others who did not have what they were indebted to pay.

For the life of that man [Jesus] is more precious than everything that is not God, and it surpasses every debt owed by sinners as satisfaction. For if putting Him to death [is a sin which] surpass- es the multitude and mag- nitude of all conceivable sins which are not against the person of God, clearly His life is a good greater than the evil of all those sins which are not against the person of God. To honor the Father, that man [Jesus]—al- though not oblig- ed to die, because not a sinner—freely gave something of His own when He permitted His life to be taken from Him for the sake of justice. [He permitted this] in order to show to all others by example that they ought not to forsake the justice of God even because of death, which inevitably they are obliged to undergo at some time or other; for He who was not obliged [to undergo] death and who, having kept justice, could have avoided death, freely and for the sake of justice endured death, which was in- flicted upon Him. Thus, in that man human nature freely and out of no obligation gave to God something its own, so that it might re- deem itself in others in whom it did not have what it, as a result of indebt- edness, was required to pay.

In all these occurrences the divine nature [in the God-man] was not abased but the human nature was exalted. The divine nature was not weakened but the human nature was mercifully assisted. Moreover, in that man the human nature did not suffer anything out of necessity but suffered only voluntarily. That man did not succumb to any compelling force; but out of voluntary goodness, and for the honor of God and the benefit of other men, He bore mercifully and laudably what was inflicted upon Him out of malev- olence. The requirement of obedience did not constrain Him, but His mighty wisdom disposed Him. For the Father by His command did not compel that man to die, but that man freely performed what He knew would please the Father and would be helpful to [other] men. The Father could not compel Him with respect to that which He ought not to have required of Him. The very great honor which the Son with such a good will freely offered to the Father could not fail to please the Father. Therefore, when the Son freely willed to do what he knew would please the Father, in this way He displayed free obedience to the Father. Furthermore, since the Father gave the Son this good will—a will nonetheless free [i.e., even though bestowed by another]—the Son is rightly said to have received this will as the Father's command. Therefore, in this way, the Son was obedient to the Father even unto death; and He did as the Father gave Him com- mandment; and He drank of the chalice which the Father gave Him.

For this is human nature's perfect and completely free obedience when [in Jesus] it freely sub- mitted its own free will to the will of God and when it freely and without any constraint exercised the good will which it had re- ceived.

Thus, that man redeemed all other men when what He freely gave to God God reckoned for the debt they owed. Through this payment a man is redeemed from his faults not once only; rather, he is received as often as he

returns again in worthy penitence. Nevertheless, this penitence is not promised to the sinner. But since [payment] was made on the cross, our Christ
has redeemed us through the cross. Therefore, those who will to come to
this grace with worthy affection are saved; but those who despise this grace
are justly condemned because they do not pay the debt they owe.

Behold, 0 Christian soul, this is the strength of your salvation, this is the
basis of your freedom, this is the cost of your redemption. You were in
bondage, but in this way you have been redeemed. You were a servant, but
in this way you have been set free. You are an exile who in this manner has
been led back home, someone lost who has been found, someone dead who
has been revived. 0 man, let your heart feed upon these thoughts, let it chew
continually upon them, let it suck upon them and swallow them whenever
your mouth receives the flesh and blood of your Redeemer. In this life
make these thoughts your daily bread, your nourishment, your provision.
For through these thoughts and only through them will you remain in
Christ and Christ in you; and only through them will your joy be full in the
life to come.

But You, 0 Lord, You who underwent death so that I might live, how can I
rejoice over my freedom, which results only from Your bonds ? How can I
be glad about my salvation when it comes only because of Your sorrows ?
How can I delight in my life, which is secured only by Your death? Shall I
rejoice over what You have suffered and over the cruelty of those who have
inflicted these sufferings upon You? For had they not done so, You would
not have suffered; and had You not suffered, I would not have possessed
these goods. On the other hand, if I grieve over Your sufferings, how can
I delight in these goods for the sake of which Your sufferings occurred
and which would not have existed had Your suf- ferings not occurred? But
surely those wicked men were not able to do anything except because You
freely permitted it; nor did You suffer except because You graciously willed
to. And so, I ought to detest the cruelty of those wicked men, to imitate
Your sufferings and death by grieving over them, to love Your gracious will
by giving thanks, and in these ways to exult, free of distress, over the
goods conferred upon me.

Therefore, 0 insignificant man, leave the cruelty of these men to the judgment of God, and meditate upon what you owe your Savior. Consider
what your condition was and what has been done for you; reflect upon how
worthy of love is He who has done this for you. Behold your need and His
goodness; see what thanks you may give and how much you owe to His
love. You were in dark- ness, on slippery footing, on the downward road
to the chaos of Hell, from which there is no return. An enormous lead-
like weight hanging from your neck was causing you to stoop. A burden
too heavy for your back was pressing upon you. Invisible foes were urging
you onward with all their fury. Such was your helplessness and you did not
know it, because you were conceived and born in that condition. 0 how desperate was that condition! To what a destination these forces were impelling
you! Let the memory of it terrify you; tremble at the very thought!

0 good Lord Jesus Christ, in this state I was neither seeking nor deliberat-
ing; but like the sun You shined forth upon me and showed me my plight.
You cast off the leaden weight which was drawing me down; You removed
the burden which was pushing me down; You repelled the foes who were
impelling me onward, ward- ing them off for my sake. You called me by a
new name which You derived from Your name. Stooped over as I was, You
stood me upright to face You, saying: "Be confident, I have redeemed You
and given my soul [life] for you. If you will cling to me, you will escape the
evils of your former condition and will not fall into the abyss toward which
you were hastening; instead, I will lead you to my kingdom and will make
you an heir of God and a joint-heir with me." Thereafter, You brought me
under Your protection so that nothing might harm my soul against its will.
And, lo, although I did not yet cling to You as You had exhorted, You still
did not permit me to fall into Hell. But You awaited the time when I would
cling to You and You would do what You had promised.

Yes, 0 Lord, such was my condition, and these things You have done for
me. I was in darkness because I knew nothing—not even my very self.
I was on slippery footing because I was weak and prone to sin. I was on
the downward road to the chaos of Hell because in our first parents I
had descended from justice to injustice (and injustice leads down to Hell),

from happiness to the misery of this life (from which one falls into eternal misery). The weight of original sin was dragging me down; the unbearable burden of God's judgment was pushing me down; demons hostile to me were urging me on, as strenuously as they could, so that they might make me deserving of even greater condemnation because of added sins. Being thus destitute of all help, I was illumined by You and shown my condition. For while I was not yet able to know my condition You taught all these things to others on my behalf; and later You taught these same things to me even before I inquired. You cast aside the leaden weight, the heavy burden, and the impelling foes, for You removed the sin in which I had been conceived and born, You removed also the condemnation of this sin, and You forbade evil spirits to constrain my soul. You gave me the name Christian, which derives from Your own name; through Your name I confess, and You acknowledge, that I am among the redeemed. You stood me upright and lifted me to the knowledge and love of You. You made me confident of my soul's salvation, for which You gave Your soul [life]. You promised me Your glory if I would follow You. And, behold, while I was not yet following You, as You had exhorted, but was even continuing to commit manifold sins, which You had proscribed, You awaited the time when I would follow You and You would give what You had promised.

Consider, 0 my soul, peer into, 0 my inmost being, how much my entire substance owes to Him. Yes, 0 Lord, because You cre- ated me I owe my entire self to Your love; because You redeemed me I owe my entire self; because Your promises are so great I owe my entire self. Indeed, I owe to Your love much more than myself—as much more as You are greater than I, for whom You gave Yourself and to whom You promise Yourself. I pray You, 0 Lord, make me to taste by loving, what I taste by knowing. Let me sense by affection what I sense by understanding. I owe more than my entire self, but I have no more to give; of myself I am not even able to give my entire self. 0 Lord, draw my whole self into Your love. The whole of what I am is Yours through Your creating; make it Yours through its loving commitment.

Behold, 0 Lord, my heart is before You. It strains, but can do nothing of itself; do, 0 Lord, what it cannot do. Receive me into the inner chamber of Your love. I ask, I seek, I knock. You who cause me to ask, cause me also to receive. You grant that I seek; grant that I also may find. You teach me to knock; open to me when I knock. If You deny to him who asks, to whom do You then give ? If he who seeks seeks in vain, who then finds? If You keep [the chamber door] closed for one who knocks, for whom do You open ? If You withhold Your love from one who implores, what do You give to one who does not implore? You cause me to desire; cause me also to obtain. 0 my soul, cling to Him, cling tenaciously. Good Lord, 0 good Lord, do not scorn my soul, which faints out of hunger for Your love. Revive my soul; let Your tender kindness satisfy it, let Your affection make it fat, let Your love fill it. Let Your love seize my whole being; let it possess me completely, because together with the Father and the Holy Spirit You are the only God, blessed forever. Amen.

THOMAS AQUINAS: SUMMA THEOLOGI- CA EXCERPT

TOP TEN THEOLOGIANS

Whether, besides philosophy, any further doctrine is required?

Objection 1: It seems that, besides philosophical science, we have no need of any further knowledge. For man should not seek to know what is above reason: "Seek not the things that are too high for thee" (Ecclus. 3:22). But whatever is not above reason is fully treated of in philosophical science. Therefore any other knowledge besides philosophical science is superfluous.

Objection 2: Further, knowledge can be concerned only with being, for nothing can be known, save what is true; and all that is, is true. But everything that is, is treated of in philosophical science---even God Himself; so that there is a part of philosophy called theology, or the divine science, as Aristotle has proved (Metaph. vi). Therefore, besides philosophical science, there is no need of any further knowledge.

On the contrary, It is written (2 Tim. 3:16): "All Scripture, inspired of God is profitable to teach, to reprove, to correct, to instruct in justice."

Now Scripture, inspired of God, is no part of philosophical science, which has been built up by human reason. Therefore it is useful that besides philosophical science, there should be other knowledge, i.e. inspired of God.

I answer that, It was necessary for man's salvation that there should be a knowledge revealed by God besides philosophical science built up by human reason. Firstly, indeed, because man is directed to God, as to an end that surpasses the grasp of his reason: "The eye hath not seen, O God, besides Thee, what things Thou hast prepared for them that wait for Thee" (Is. 66:4). But the end must first be known by men who are to direct their thoughts and actions to the end. Hence it was necessary for the salvation of man that certain truths which exceed human reason should be made known to him by divine revelation. Even as regards those truths about God which human reason could have discovered, it was necessary that man should be taught by a divine revelation; because the truth about God such as reason could discover, would only be known by a few, and that after a long time, and with the admixture of many errors. Whereas man's whole salvation, which is in God, depends upon the knowledge of this truth. Therefore, in order that the salvation of men might be brought about more fitly and more surely, it was necessary that they should be taught divine truths by divine revelation. It was therefore necessary that besides philosophical science built up by reason, there should be a sacred science learned through revelation.

Reply to Objection 1: Although those things which are beyond man's knowledge may not be sought for by man through his reason, nevertheless, once they are revealed by God, they must be accepted by faith. Hence the sacred text continues, "For many things are shown to thee above the understanding of man" (Ecclus. 3:25). And in this, the sacred science consists.

Reply to Objection 2: Sciences are differentiated according to the various means through which knowledge is obtained. For the astronomer and the physicist both may prove the same conclusion: that the earth, for instance, is round: the astronomer by means of mathematics (i.e. abstracting from matter), but the physicist by means of matter itself. Hence there is no reason why those things which may be learned from philosophical science, so far as they can be known by natural reason, may not also be taught us by another science so far as they fall within revelation. Hence theology included in sacred doctrine differs in kind from that theology which is part of philosophy.

Whether God is truth?

Objection 1: It seems that God is not truth. For truth consists in the intellect composing and dividing. But in God there is not composition and division. Therefore in Him there is not truth.

Objection 2: Further, truth, according to Augustine (De Vera Relig. xxxvi) is a "likeness to the principle." But in God there is no likeness to a principle. Therefore in God there is not truth.

Objection 3: Further, whatever is said of God, is said of Him as of the first cause of all things; thus the being of God is the cause of all being; and His goodness the cause of all good. If therefore there is truth in God, all truth will be from Him. But it is true that someone sins. Therefore this will be from God; which is evidently false.

On the contrary, Our Lord says, "I am the Way, the Truth, and the Life" (Jn. 14:6).

I answer that, As said above (A[1]), truth is found in the intellect according as it apprehends a thing as it is; and in things according as they have being conformable to an intellect. This is to the greatest degree found in God. For His being is not only conformed to His intellect, but it is the very act of His intellect; and His act of understanding is the measure and cause of every other being and of every other intellect, and He Himself is His own existence and act of understanding. Whence it follows not only that truth is in Him, but that He is truth itself, and the sovereign and first truth.

Reply to Objection 1: Although in the divine intellect there is neither composition nor division, yet in His simple act of intelligence He judges of all things and knows all things complex; and thus there is truth in His intellect.

Reply to Objection 2: The truth of our intellect is according to its conformity with its principle, that is to say, to the things from which it receives knowledge. The truth also of things is according to their conformity with their principle, namely, the divine intellect. Now this cannot be said, properly speaking, of divine truth; unless perhaps in so far as truth is appropriated to the Son, Who has a principle. But if we speak of divine truth in its essence, we cannot understand this unless the affirmative must be resolved into the negative, as when one says: "the Father is of Himself, because He is not from another." Similarly, the divine truth can be called a "likeness to the principle," inasmuch as His existence is not dissimilar to His intellect.

Reply to Objection 3: Not-being and privation have no truth of themselves, but only in the apprehension of the intellect. Now all apprehension of the intellect is from God. Hence all the truth that exists in the statement--"that a person commits fornication is true"---is entirely from God. But to argue, "Therefore that this person fornicates is from God", is a fallacy of Accident.

RESOLUTIONS OF JONTHAN EDWARDS 1723AD

TOP TEN THEOLOGIANS

Being sensible that I am unable to do anything without God's help, I do humbly entreat him by his grace to enable me to keep these Resolutions, so far as they are agreeable to his will, for Christ's sake.

Remember to read over these Resolutions once a week.

Overall Life Mission

1. Resolved, that I will do whatsoever I think to be most to God's glory, and my own good, profit and pleasure, in the whole of my duration, without any consideration of the time, whether now, or never so many myriad's of ages hence. Resolved to do whatever I think to be my duty and most for the good and advantage of mankind in general. Resolved to do this, whatever difficulties I meet with, how many and how great soever.

2. Resolved, to be continually endeavoring to find out some new invention and contrivance to promote the aforementioned things.

3. Resolved, if ever I shall fall and grow dull, so as to neglect to keep any

part of these Resolutions, to repent of all I can remember, when I come to myself again.

4. Resolved, never to do any manner of thing, whether in soul or body, less or more, but what tends to the glory of God; nor be, nor suffer it, if I can avoid it.

6. Resolved, to live with all my might, while I do live.

22. Resolved, to endeavor to obtain for myself as much happiness, in the other world, as I possibly can, with all the power; might, vigor, and vehemence, yea violence, I am capable of, or can bring myself to exert, in any way that can be thought of.

62. Resolved, never to do anything but duty; and then according to Eph. 6:6-8, do it willingly and cheerfully as unto the Lord, and not to man; "knowing that whatever good thing any man doth, the same shall he receive of the Lord." June 25 and July 13, 1723.

Good Works

11. Resolved, when I think of any theorem in divinity to be solved, immediately to do what I can towards solving it, if circumstances don't hinder.

13. Resolved, to be endeavoring to find out fit objects of charity and liberality.

69. Resolved, always to do that, which I shall wish I had done when I see others do it. Aug. 11, 1723.

Time Management

5. Resolved, never to lose one moment of time; but improve it the most profitable way I possibly can.

7. Resolved, never to do anything, which I should be afraid to do, if it were the last hour of my life.

17. Resolved, that I will live so as I shall wish I had done when I come to die.

18. Resolved, to live so at all times, as I think is best in my devout frames, and when I have clearest notions of things of the gospel, and another world.

19. Resolved, never to do anything, which I should be afraid to do, if I expected it would not be above an hour, before I should hear the last trump.

37. Resolved, to inquire every night, as I am going to bed, wherein I have been negligent, what sin I have committed, and wherein I have denied myself: also at the end of every week, month and year. Dec. 22 and 26, 1722.

40. Resolved, to inquire every night, before I go to bed, whether I have acted in the best way I possibly could, with respect to eating and drinking. Jan. 7, 1723.

41. Resolved, to ask myself at the end of every day, week, month and year, wherein I could possibly in any respect have done better. Jan. 11, 1723.

50.Resolved, I will act so as I think I shall judge would have been best, and most prudent, when I come into the future world. July 5, 1723.

51.Resolved, that I will act so, in every respect, as I think I shall wish I had done, if I should at last be damned. July 8, 1723.

52. I frequently hear persons in old age say how they would live, if they were to live their lives over again: Resolved, that I will live just so as I can think I shall wish I had done, supposing I live to old age. July 8, 1723.

55. Resolved, to endeavor to my utmost to act as I can think I should do, if I had already seen the happiness of heaven, and hell torments. July 8, 1723.

61. Resolved, that I will not give way to that listlessness which I find unbends and relaxes my mind from being fully and fixedly set on religion, whatever excuse I may have for it-that what my listlessness inclines me to do, is best to be done, etc. May 21, and July 13, 1723.

Relationships

14. Resolved, never to do anything out of revenge.

15. Resolved, never to suffer the least motions of anger to irrational beings.

16. Resolved, never to speak evil of anyone, so that it shall tend to his dishonor, more or less, upon no account except for some real good.

31. Resolved, never to say anything at all against anybody, but when it is perfectly agreeable to the highest degree of Christian honor, and of love to mankind, agreeable to the lowest humility, and sense of my own faults and failings, and agreeable to the golden rule; often, when I have said anything against anyone, to bring it to, and try it strictly by the test of this Resolution.

33. Resolved, always to do what I can towards making, maintaining, establishing and preserving peace, when it can be without over-balancing detriment in other respects. Dec. 26, 1722.

34. Resolved, in narration's never to speak anything but the pure and simple verity.

36. Resolved, never to speak evil of any, except I have some particular good call for it. Dec. 19, 1722.

46. Resolved, never to allow the least measure of any fretting uneasiness at my father or mother. Resolved to suffer no effects of it, so much as in the least alteration of speech, or motion of my eve: and to be especially careful of it, with respect to any of our family.

58. Resolved, not only to refrain from an air of dislike, fretfulness, and anger in conversation, but to exhibit an air of love, cheerfulness and benignity. May 27, and July 13, 1723.

59. Resolved, when I am most conscious of provocations to ill nature and anger, that I will strive most to feel and act good-naturedly; yea, at such times, to manifest good nature, though I think that in other respects it would be disadvantageous, and so as would be imprudent at other times. May 12, July 2, and July 13.

66. Resolved, that I will endeavor always to keep a benign aspect, and air of acting and speaking in all places, and in all companies, except it should so happen that duty requires otherwise.

70. Let there be something of benevolence, in all that I speak.

Suffering

9. Resolved, to think much on all occasions of my own dying, and of the common circumstances which attend death.

10. Resolved, when I feel pain, to think of the pains of martyrdom, and of hell.

67. Resolved, after afflictions, to inquire, what I am the better for them, what good I have got by them, and what I might have got by them.

57. Resolved, when I fear misfortunes and adversities, to examine whether ~ have done my duty, and resolve to do it; and let it be just as providence

orders it, I will as far as I can, be concerned about nothing but my duty and my sin. June 9, and July 13, 1723.

Character

8. Resolved, to act, in all respects, both speaking and doing, as if nobody had been so vile as I, and as if I had committed the same sins, or had the same infirmities or failings as others; and that I will let the knowledge of their failings promote nothing but shame in myself, and prove only an occasion of my confessing my own sins and misery to God.

12. Resolved, if I take delight in it as a gratification of pride, or vanity, or on any such account, immediately to throw it by.

21. Resolved, never to do anything, which if I should see in another, I should count a just occasion to despise him for, or to think any way the more meanly of him.

32. Resolved, to be strictly and firmly faithful to my trust, that that in Prov. 20:6, "A faithful man who can find?" may not be partly fulfilled in me.

47. Resolved, to endeavor to my utmost to deny whatever is not most agreeable to a good, and universally sweet and benevolent, quiet, peaceable, contented, easy, compassionate, generous, humble, meek, modest, submissive, obliging, diligent and industrious, charitable, even, patient, moderate, forgiving, sincere temper; and to do at all times what such a temper would lead me to. Examine strictly every week, whether I have done so. Sabbath morning. May 5, 1723.

54. Whenever I hear anything spoken in conversation of any person, if I think it would be praiseworthy in me, Resolved to endeavor to imitate it. July 8, 1723.

63. On the supposition, that there never was to be but one individual in the world, at any one time, who was properly a complete Christian, in all re-

spects of a right stamp, having Christianity always shining in its true luster, and appearing excellent and lovely, from whatever part and under whatever character viewed: Resolved, to act just as I would do, if I strove with all my might to be that one, who should live in my time. Jan. 14 and July 3, 1723.

27. Resolved, never willfully to omit anything, except the omission be for the glory of God; and frequently to examine my omissions.

39. Resolved, never to do anything that I so much question the lawfulness of, as that I intend, at the same time, to consider and examine afterwards, whether it be lawful or no; except I as much question the lawfulness of the omission.

20. Resolved, to maintain the strictest temperance in eating and drinking.

Spiritual Life

Assurance

25. Resolved, to examine carefully, and constantly, what that one thing in me is, which causes me in the least to doubt of the love of God; and to direct all my forces against it.

26. Resolved, to cast away such things, as I find do abate my assurance.

48. Resolved, constantly, with the utmost niceness and diligence, and the strictest scrutiny, to be looking into the state of my soul, that I may know whether I have truly an interest in Christ or no; that when I come to die, I may not have any negligence respecting this to repent of. May 26, 1723.

49. Resolved, that this never shall be, if I can help it.

The Scriptures

28. Resolved, to study the Scriptures so steadily, constantly and frequent-

ly, as that I may find, and plainly perceive myself to grow in the knowledge of the same.

Prayer

29. Resolved, never to count that a prayer, nor to let that pass as a prayer, nor that as a petition of a prayer, which is so made, that I cannot hope that God will answer it; nor that as a confession, which I cannot hope God will accept.

64. Resolved, when I find those "groanings which cannot be uttered" (Rom. 8:26), of which the Apostle speaks, and those "breakings of soul for the longing it hath," of which the Psalmist speaks, Psalm 119:20, that I will promote them to the utmost of my power, and that I will not be wear', of earnestly endeavoring to vent my desires, nor of the repetitions of such earnestness. July 23, and August 10, 1723.

The Lord's Day

38. Resolved, never to speak anything that is ridiculous, sportive, or matter of laughter on the Lord's day. Sabbath evening, Dec. 23, 1722.

Vivification of Righteousness

30. Resolved, to strive to my utmost every week to be brought higher in religion, and to a higher exercise of grace, than I was the week before.

42. Resolved, frequently to renew the dedication of myself to God, which was made at my baptism; which I solemnly renewed, when I was received into the communion of the church; and which I have solemnly re-made this twelfth day of January, 1722-23.

43. Resolved, never henceforward, till I die, to act as if I were any way my own, but entirely and altogether God's, agreeable to what is to be found in Saturday, January 12, 1723.

44- Resolved, that no other end but religion, shall have any influence at all on any of my actions; and that no action shall be, in the least circumstance, any otherwise than the religious end will carry it. Jan.12, 1723.

45. Resolved, never to allow any pleasure or grief, joy or sorrow, nor any affection at all, nor any degree of affection, nor any circumstance relating to it, but what helps religion. Jan. 12-13, 1723.

Mortification of Sin and Self Examination

23. Resolved, frequently to take some deliberate action, which seems most unlikely to be done, for the glory of God, and trace it back to the original intention, designs and ends of it; and if I find it not to be for God's glory, to repute it as a breach of the 4th Resolution.

24. Resolved, whenever I do any conspicuously evil action, to trace it back, till I come to the original cause; and then both carefully endeavor to do so no more, and to fight and pray with all my might against the original of it.

35. Resolved, whenever I so much question whether I have done my duty, as that my quiet and calm is thereby disturbed, to set it down, and also how the question was resolved. Dec. 18, 1722.

60. Resolved, whenever my feelings begin to appear in the least out of order, when I am conscious of the least uneasiness within, or the least irregularity without, I will then subject myself to the strictest examination. July 4 and 13, 1723.

68. Resolved, to confess frankly to myself all that which I find in myself, either infirmity or sin; and, if it be what concerns religion, also to confess the whole case to God, and implore needed help. July 23 and August 10, 1723.

56. Resolved, never to give over, nor in the least to slacken my fight with my corruptions, however unsuccessful I may be.

Communion with God

53. Resolved, to improve every opportunity, when I am in the best and happiest frame of mind, to cast and venture my soul on the Lord Jesus Christ, to trust and confide in him, and consecrate myself wholly to him; that from this I may have assurance of my safety, knowing that I confide in my Redeemer. July 8, 1723.

65. Resolved, very much to exercise myself in this all my life long, viz. with the greatest openness I am capable of, to declare my ways to God, and lay open my soul to him: all my sins, temptations, difficulties, sorrows, fears, hopes, desires, and every thing, and every circumstance; according to Dr. Manton's 27th Sermon on Psalm 119. July 26 and Aug. 10, 1723.

Aug. 17, 1723

ATHANASIUS ON THE INCARNATION EXCERPT - 318AD

TOP TEN THEOLOGIANS

The Divine Dilemma and Its Solution in the Incarnation

We saw in the last chapter that, because death and corruption were gaining ever firmer hold on them, the human race was in process of destruction. Man, who was created in God's image and in his possession of reason reflected the very Word Himself, was disappearing, and the work of God was being undone. The law of death, which followed from the Transgression, prevailed upon us, and from it there was no escape. The thing that was happening was in truth both monstrous and unfitting. It would, of course, have been unthinkable that God should go back upon His word and that man, having transgressed, should not die; but it was equally monstrous that beings which once had shared the nature of the Word should perish and turn back again into non-existence through corruption. It was unworthy of the goodness of God that creatures made by Him should be brought to nothing through the deceit wrought upon man by the devil; and it was supremely unfitting that the work of God in mankind should disappear, either through their own negligence or through the deceit of evil spirits. As, then, the creatures whom He had created reasonable, like the Word, were in fact perishing, and such noble works were on the road to ruin, what then was God, being Good, to do? Was He to let corruption and death have their way with them? In that case, what was the use of having made them in the beginning? Surely it would have been better never to have been created at all than, having been created, to be neglected and perish; and, besides that, such indifference to the ruin of His own work before His very eyes would argue not goodness in God but limitation, and that far more than if He had never created men at all. It was impossible, therefore, that God should leave man to be carried off by corruption, because it would be unfitting and unworthy of Himself.

(7) Yet, true though this is, it is not the whole matter. As we have already noted, it was unthinkable that God, the Father of Truth, should go back upon His word regarding death in order to ensure our continued existence. He could not falsify Himself; what, then, was God to do? Was He to demand repentance from men for their transgression? You might say that that was worthy of God, and argue further that, as through the Transgression they became subject to corruption, so through repentance they might return to incorruption again. But repentance would not guard the Divine consistency, for, if death did not hold dominion over men, God would still remain untrue. Nor does repentance recall men from what is according to their nature; all that it does is to make them cease from sinning. Had it been a case of a trespass only, and not of a subsequent corruption, repentance would have been well enough; but when once transgression had begun men came under the power of the corruption proper to their nature and were bereft of the grace which belonged to them as creatures in the Image of God. No, repentance could not meet the case. What—or rather Who was it that was needed for such grace and such recall as we required? Who, save the Word of God Himself, Who also in the beginning had made all things out of nothing? His part it was, and His alone, both to bring again the corruptible to incorruption and to maintain for the Father His consistency of character with all. For He alone, being Word of the Father and above all, was in consequence both able to recreate all, and worthy to suffer on behalf of all and to be an ambassador for all with the Father.

(8) For this purpose, then, the incorporeal and incorruptible and immaterial Word of God entered our world. In one sense, indeed, He was not far from it before, for no part of creation had ever been without Him Who, while ever abiding in union with the Father, yet fills all things that are. But now He entered the world in a new way, stooping to our level in His love and Self-revealing to us. He saw the reasonable race, the race of men that, like Himself, expressed the Father's Mind, wasting out of existence, and death reigning over all in corruption. He saw that corruption held us all the closer, because it was the penalty for the Transgression; He saw, too, how unthinkable it would be for the law to be repealed before it was fulfilled. He saw how unseemly it was that the very things of which He Himself was the Artificer should be disappearing. He saw how the surpassing wickedness of men was mounting up against them; He saw also their universal liability to death. All this He saw and, pitying our race, moved with compassion for our limitation, unable to endure that death should have the mastery, rather than that His creatures should perish and the work of His Father for us men come to nought, He took to Himself a body, a human body even as our own. Nor did He will merely to become embodied or merely to appear; had that been so, He could have revealed His divine majesty in some other and better way. No, He took our body, and not only so, but He took it directly from a spotless, stainless virgin, without the agency of human father—a pure body, untainted by intercourse with man. He, the Mighty One, the Artificer of all, Himself prepared this body in the virgin as a temple for Himself, and took it for His very own, as the instrument through which He was known and in which He dwelt. Thus, taking a body like our own, because all our bodies were liable to the corruption of death, He surrendered His body to death instead of all, and offered it to the Father. This He did out of sheer love for us, so that in His death all might die, and the law of death thereby be abolished because, having fulfilled in His body that for which it was appointed, it was thereafter voided of its power for men. This He did that He might turn again to incorruption men who had turned back to corruption, and make them alive through death by the appropriation of His body and by the grace of His resurrection. Thus He would make death to disappear from them as utterly as straw from fire.

(9) The Word perceived that corruption could not be got rid of otherwise than through death; yet He Himself, as the Word, being immortal and the Father's Son, was such as could not die. For this reason, therefore, He assumed a body capable of death, in order that it, through belonging to the Word Who is above all, might become in dying a sufficient exchange for all, and, itself remaining incorruptible through His indwelling, might thereafter put an end to corruption for all others as well, by the grace of the resurrection. It was by surrendering to death the body which He had taken, as an offering and sacrifice free from every stain, that He forthwith abolished death for His human brethren by the offering of the equivalent. For naturally, since the Word of God was above all, when He offered His own temple and bodily instrument as a substitute for the life of all, He fulfilled in death all that was required. Naturally also, through this union of the immortal Son of God with our human nature, all men were clothed with incorruption in the promise of the resurrection. For the solidarity of mankind is such that, by virtue of the Word's indwelling in a single human body, the corruption which goes with death has lost its power over all. You know how it is when some great king enters a large city and dwells in one of its houses; because of his dwelling in that single house, the whole city is honored, and enemies and robbers cease to molest it. Even so is it with the King of all; He has come into our country and dwelt in one body amidst the many, and in consequence the designs of the enemy against mankind have been foiled and the corruption of death, which formerly held them in its power, has simply ceased to be. For the human race would have perished utterly had not the Lord and Savior of all, the Son of God, come among us to put an end to death.

(10) This great work was, indeed, supremely worthy of the goodness of God. A king who has founded a city, so far from neglecting it when through the carelessness of the inhabitants it is attacked by robbers, avenges it and saves it from destruction, having regard rather to his own honor than to the people's neglect. Much more, then, the Word of the All-good Father was not unmindful of the human race that He had called to be; but rather, by the offering of His own body He abolished the death which they had incurred, and corrected their neglect by His own teaching. Thus by His own

power He restored the whole nature of man. The Savior's own inspired disciples assure us of this. We read in one place: " For the love of Christ constraineth us, because we thus judge that, if One died on behalf of all, then all died, and He died for all that we should no longer live unto ourselves, but unto Him who died and rose again from the dead, even our Lord Jesus Christ."[1] And again another says: "But we behold Him Who hath been made a little lower than the angels, even Jesus, because of the suffering of death crowned with glory and honor, that by the grace of God He should taste of death on behalf of every man." The same writer goes on to point out why it was necessary for God the Word and none other to become Man: "For it became Him, for Whom are all things and through Whom are all things, in bringing many sons unto glory, to make the Author of their salvation perfect through suffering.[2] He means that the rescue of mankind from corruption was the proper part only of Him Who made them in the beginning. He points out also that the Word assumed a human body, expressly in order that He might offer it in sacrifice for other like bodies: "Since then the children are sharers in flesh and blood, He also Himself assumed the same, in order that through death He might bring to nought Him that hath the power of death, that is to say, the Devil, and might rescue those who all their lives were enslaved by the fear of death."[3] For by the sacrifice of His own body He did two things: He put an end to the law of death which barred our way; and He made a new beginning of life for us, by giving us the hope of resurrection. By man death has gained its power over men; by the Word made Man death has been destroyed and life raised up anew. That is what Paul says, that true servant of Christ: For since by man came death, by man came also the resurrection of the dead. Just as in Adam all die, even so in Christ shall all be made alive,"[4] and so forth. Now, therefore, when we die we no longer do so as men condemned to death, but as those who are even now in process of rising we await the general resurrection of all, "which in its own times He shall show,"[5] even God Who wrought it and bestowed it on us.

This, then, is the first cause of the Savior's becoming Man. There are, however, other things which show how wholly fitting is His blessed presence in our midst; and these we must now go on to consider.

The Divine Dilemma and Its Solution in the Incarnation—continued

When God the Almighty was making mankind through His own Word, He perceived that they, owing to the limitation of their nature, could not of themselves have any knowledge of their Artificer, the Incorporeal and Uncreated. He took pity on them, therefore, and did not leave them destitute of the knowledge of Himself, lest their very existence should prove purposeless. For of what use is existence to the creature if it cannot know its Maker? How could men be reasonable beings if they had no knowledge of the Word and Reason of the Father, through Whom they had received their being? They would be no better than the beasts, had they no knowledge save of earthly things; and why should God have made them at all, if He had not intended them to know Him? But, in fact, the good God has given them a share in His own Image, that is, in our Lord Jesus Christ, and has made even themselves after the same Image and Likeness. Why? Simply in order that through this gift of Godlikeness in themselves they may be able to perceive the Image Absolute, that is the Word Himself, and through Him to apprehend the Father; which knowledge of their Maker is for men the only really happy and blessed life.

But, as we have already seen, men, foolish as they are, thought little of the grace they had received, and turned away from God. They defiled their own soul so completely that they not only lost their apprehension of God, but invented for themselves other gods of various kinds. They fashioned idols for themselves in place of the truth and reverenced things that are not, rather than God Who is, as St. Paul says, "worshipping the creature rather than the Creator."[1] Moreover, and much worse, they transferred the honor which is due to God to material objects such as wood and stone, and also to man; and further even than that they went, as we said in our former book. Indeed, so impious were they that they worshiped evil spirits as gods in satisfaction of their lusts. They sacrificed brute beasts and immolated men, as the just due of these deities, thereby bringing themselves more and more under their insane control. Magic arts also were taught among them, oracles in sundry places led men astray, and the cause of everything in human life was traced to the stars as though nothing existed but that which could be seen. In a word, impiety and lawlessness were everywhere, and neither God nor His Word was known. Yet He had not hidden Himself from the sight of men nor given the knowledge of Himself in one way only; but rather He had unfolded it in many forms and by many ways.

(12) God knew the limitation of mankind, you see; and though the grace of being made in His Image was sufficient to give them knowledge of the Word and through Him of the Father, as a safeguard against their neglect of this grace, He provided the works of creation also as means by which the Maker might be known. Nor was this all. Man's neglect of the indwelling grace tends ever to increase; and against this further frailty also God made provision by giving them a law, and by sending prophets, men whom they knew. Thus, if they were tardy in looking up to heaven, they might still gain knowledge of their Maker from those close at hand; for men can learn directly about higher things from other men. Three ways thus lay open to them, by which they might obtain the knowledge of God. They could look up into the immensity of heaven, and by pondering the harmony of creation come to know its Ruler, the Word of the Father, Whose all-ruling providence makes known the Father to all. Or, if this was beyond them, they could converse with holy men, and through them learn to know God, the Artificer of all things, the Father of Christ, and to recognize the worship of idols as the negation of the truth and full of all impiety. Or else, in the third place, they could cease from lukewarmness and lead a good life merely by knowing the law. For the law was not given only for the Jews, nor was it solely for their sake that God sent the prophets, though it was to the Jews that they were sent and by the Jews that they were persecuted. The law and the prophets were a sacred school of the knowledge of God and the conduct of the spiritual life for the whole world.

So great, indeed, were the goodness and the love of God. Yet men, bowed down by the pleasures of the moment and by the frauds and illusions of the evil spirits, did not lift up their heads towards the truth. So burdened were they with their wickednesses that they seemed rather to be brute beasts than reasonable men, reflecting the very Likeness of the Word.

(13) What was God to do in face of this dehumanising of mankind, this universal hiding of the knowledge of Himself by the wiles of evil spirits? Was He to keep silence before so great a wrong and let men go on being thus deceived and kept in ignorance of Himself? If so, what was the use of having made them in His own Image originally? It would surely have been better for them always to have been brutes, rather than to revert to that condition when once they had shared the nature of the Word. Again, things being as they were, what was the use of their ever having had the knowledge of God? Surely it would have been better for God never to have bestowed it, than that men should subsequently be found unworthy to receive it. Similarly, what possible profit could it be to God Himself, Who made men, if when made they did not worship Him, but regarded others as their makers? This would be tantamount to His having made them for others and not for Himself. Even an earthly king, though he is only a man, does not allow lands that he has colonized to pass into other hands or to desert to other rulers, but sends letters and friends and even visits them himself to recall them to their allegiance, rather than allow His work to be undone. How much more, then, will God be patient and painstaking with His creatures, that they be not led astray from Him to the service of those that are not, and that all the more because such error means for them sheer ruin, and because it is not right that those who had once shared His Image should be destroyed.

What, then, was God to do? What else could He possibly do, being God, but renew His Image in mankind, so that through it men might once more come to know Him? And how could this be done save by the coming of the very Image Himself, our Savior Jesus Christ? Men could not have done it, for they are only made after the Image; nor could angels have done it, for they are not the images of God. The Word of God came in His own Person, because it was He alone, the Image of the Father Who could recreate man made after the Image.

In order to effect this re-creation, however, He had first to do away with death and corruption. Therefore He assumed a human body, in order that in it death might once for all be destroyed, and that men might be renewed according to the Image. The Image of the Father only was sufficient for this need. Here is an illustration to prove it.

(14) You know what happens when a portrait that has been painted on a panel becomes obliterated through external stains. The artist does not throw away the panel, but the subject of the portrait has to come and sit for it again, and then the likeness is re-drawn on the same material. Even so was it with the All-holy Son of God. He, the Image of the Father, came and dwelt in our midst, in order that He might renew mankind made after Himself, and seek out His lost sheep, even as He says in the Gospel: "I came to seek and to save that which was lost.[2] This also explains His saying to the Jews: "Except a man be born anew . . ."[3] a He was not referring to a man's natural birth from his mother, as they thought, but to the re-birth and re-creation of the soul in the Image of God.

Nor was this the only thing which only the Word could do. When the madness of idolatry and irreligion filled the world and the knowledge of God was hidden, whose part was it to teach the world about the Father? Man's, would you say? But men cannot run everywhere over the world, nor would their words carry sufficient weight if they did, nor would they be, unaided, a match for the evil spirits. Moreover, since even the best of men were confused and blinded by evil, how could they convert the souls and minds of others? You cannot put straight in others what is warped in yourself. Perhaps you will say, then, that creation was enough to teach men about the Father. But if that had been so, such great evils would never have occurred. Creation was there all the time, but it did not prevent men from wallowing in error. Once more, then, it was the Word of God, Who sees all that is in man and moves all things in creation, Who alone could meet the needs of the situation. It was His part and His alone, Whose ordering of the universe reveals the Father, to renew the same teaching. But how was He to do it? By the same means as before, perhaps you will say, that is, through the works of creation. But this was proven insufficient. Men had neglected to consider the heavens before, and now they were looking in the opposite direction.

Wherefore, in all naturalness and fitness. desiring to do good to men, as Man He dwells, taking to Himself a body like the rest; and through His actions done in that body, as it were on their own level, He teaches those who would not learn by other means to know Himself, the Word of God, and through Him the Father.

(15) He deals with them as a good teacher with his pupils, coming down to their level and using simple means. St. Paul says as much: "Because in the wisdom of God the world in its wisdom knew not God, God thought fit through the simplicity of the News proclaimed to save those who believe."[4] Men had turned from the contemplation of God above, and were looking for Him in the opposite direction, down among created things and things of sense. The Savior of us all, the Word of God, in His great love took to Himself a body and moved as Man among men, meeting their senses, so to speak, half way. He became Himself an object for the senses, so that those who were seeking God in sensible things might apprehend the Father through the works which He, the Word of God, did in the body. Human and human minded as men were, therefore, to whichever side they looked in the sensible world they found themselves taught the truth. Were they awe-stricken by creation? They beheld it confessing Christ as Lord. Did their minds tend to regard men as Gods? The uniqueness of the Savior's works marked Him, alone of men, as Son of God. Were they drawn to evil spirits? They saw them driven out by the Lord and learned that the Word of God alone was God and that the evil spirits were not gods at all. Were they inclined to hero-worship and the cult of the dead? Then the fact that the Savior had risen from the dead showed them how false these other deities were, and that the Word of the Father is the one true Lord, the Lord even of death. For this reason was He both born and manifested as Man, for this He died and rose, in order that, eclipsing by His works all other human deeds, He might recall men from all the paths of error to know the Father. As He says Himself, "I came to seek and to save that which was lost."[5] (16) When, then, the minds of men had fallen finally to the level of sensible things, the Word submitted to appear in a body, in order that He, as Man, might center their senses on Himself, and convince them through His human acts that He Himself is not man only but also God, the Word and

Wisdom of the true God. This is what Paul wants to tell us when he says: "That ye, being rooted and grounded in love, may be strong to apprehend with all the saints what is the length and breadth and height and depth, and to know the love of God that surpasses knowledge, so that ye may be filled unto all the fullness of God."[6] The Self-revealing of the Word is in every dimension—above, in creation; below, in the Incarnation; in the depth, in Hades; in the breadth, throughout the world. All things have been filled with the knowledge of God.

For this reason He did not offer the sacrifice on behalf of all immediately He came, for if He had surrendered His body to death and then raised it again at once He would have ceased to be an object of our senses. Instead of that, He stayed in His body and let Himself be seen in it, doing acts and giving signs which showed Him to be not only man, but also God the Word. There were thus two things which the Savior did for us by becoming Man. He banished death from us and made us anew; and, invisible and imperceptible as in Himself He is, He became visible through His works and revealed Himself as the Word of the Father, the Ruler and King of the whole creation.

(17) There is a paradox in this last statement which we must now examine. The Word was not hedged in by His body, nor did His presence in the body prevent His being present elsewhere as well. When He moved His body He did not cease also to direct the universe by His Mind and might. No. The marvelous truth is, that being the Word, so far from being Himself contained by anything, He actually contained all things Himself. In creation He is present everywhere, yet is distinct in being from it; ordering, directing, giving life to all, containing all, yet is He Himself the Uncontained, existing solely in His Father. As with the whole, so also is it with the part. Existing in a human body, to which He Himself gives life, He is still Source of life to all the universe, present in every part of it, yet outside the whole; and He is revealed both through the works of His body and through His activity in the world. It is, indeed, the function of soul to behold things that are outside the body, but it cannot energize or move them. A man cannot transport things from one place to another, for instance, merely by think-

ing about them; nor can you or I move the sun and the stars just by sitting at home and looking at them. With the Word of God in His human nature, however, it was otherwise. His body was for Him not a limitation, but an instrument, so that He was both in it and in all things, and outside all things, resting in the Father alone. At one and the same time—this is the wonder—as Man He was living a human life, and as Word He was sustaining the life of the universe, and as Son He was in constant union with the Father. Not even His birth from a virgin, therefore, changed Him in any way, nor was He defiled by being in the body. Rather, He sanctified the body by being in it. For His being in everything does not mean that He shares the nature of everything, only that He gives all things their being and sustains them in it. Just as the sun is not defiled by the contact of its rays with earthly objects, but rather enlightens and purifies them, so He Who made the sun is not defiled by being made known in a body, but rather the body is cleansed and quickened by His indwelling, "Who did no sin, neither was guile found in His mouth."[7]

(18) You must understand, therefore, that when writers on this sacred theme speak of Him as eating and drinking and being born, they mean that the body, as a body, was born and sustained with the food proper to its nature; while God the Word, Who was united with it, was at the same time ordering the universe and revealing Himself through His bodily acts as not man only but God. Those acts are rightly said to be His acts, because the body which did them did indeed belong to Him and none other; moreover, it was right that they should be thus attributed to Him as Man, in order to show that His body was a real one and not merely an appearance. From such ordinary acts as being born and taking food, He was recognized as being actually present in the body; but by the extraordinary acts which He did through the body He proved Himself to be the Son of God. That is the meaning of His words to the unbelieving Jews: "If I do not the works of My Father, believe Me not; but if I do, even if ye believe not Me, believe My works, that ye may know that the Father is in Me and I in the Father." Invisible in Himself, He is known from the works of creation; so also, when His Godhead is veiled in human nature, His bodily acts still declare Him to be not man only, but the Power and Word of God. To speak authoritatively

to evil spirits, for instance, and to drive them out, is not human but divine; and who could see-Him curing all the diseases to which mankind is prone, and still deem Him mere man and not also God? He cleansed lepers, He made the lame to walk, He opened the ears of the deaf and the eyes of the blind, there was no sickness or weakness that-He did not drive away. Even the most casual observer can see that these were acts of God. The healing of the man born blind, for instance, who but the Father and Artificer of man, the Controller of his whole being, could thus have restored the faculty denied at birth? He Who did thus must surely be Himself the Lord of birth. This is proved also at the outset of His becoming Man. He formed His own body from the virgin; and that is no small proof of His Godhead, since He Who made that was the Maker of all else. And would not anyone infer from the fact of that body being begotten of a virgin only, without human father, that He Who appeared in it was also the Maker and Lord of all beside?

Again, consider the miracle at Cana. Would not anyone who saw the substance of water transmuted into wine understand that He Who did it was the Lord and Maker of the water that He changed? It was for the same reason that He walked on the sea as on dry land—to prove to the onlookers that He had mastery over all. And the feeding of the multitude, when He made little into much, so that from five loaves five thousand mouths were filled—did not that prove Him none other than the very Lord Whose Mind is over all?

CALVIN'S INSTITUTES BOOK III EXCERPTS WRITTEN MID-1500'S

CHAPTER 8: OF BEARING THE CROSS—ONE BRANCH OF SELF-DENIAL.

1. The pious mind must ascend still higher, namely, whither Christ calls his disciples when he says, that every one of them must "take up his cross," (Mt. 16:24). Those whom the Lord has chosen and honoured with his intercourse must prepare for a hard, laborious, troubled life, a life full of many and various kinds of evils; it being the will of our heavenly Father to exercise his people in this way while putting them to the proof. Having begun this course with Christ the first-born, he continues it towards all his children. For though that Son was dear to him above others, the Son in whom he was "well pleased," yet we see, that far from being treated gently and indulgently, we may say, that not only was he subjected to a perpetual cross while he dwelt on earth, but his whole life was nothing else than a kind of perpetual cross. The Apostle assigns the reason, "Though he was a Son, yet learned he obedience by the things which he suffered," (Heb. 5:8). Why then should we exempt ourselves 2017from that condition to

which Christ our Head behoved to submit; especially since he submitted on our account, that he might in his own person exhibit a model of patience? Wherefore, the Apostle declares, that all the children of God are destined to be conformed to him. Hence it affords us great consolation in hard and difficult circumstances, which men deem evil and adverse, to think that we are holding fellowship with the sufferings of Christ; that as he passed to celestial glory through a labyrinth of many woes, so we too are conducted thither through various tribulations. For, in another passage, Paul himself thus speaks, "we must through much tribulation enter the kingdom of God," (Acts 14:22); and again, "that I may know him, and the power of his resurrection, and the fellowship of his sufferings, being made conformable unto his death," (Rom 8:29). How powerfully should it soften the bitterness of the cross, to think that the more we are afflicted with adversity, the surer we are made of our fellowship with Christ; by communion with whom our sufferings are not only blessed to us, but tend greatly to the furtherance of our salvation.

2. We may add, that the only thing which made it necessary for our Lord to undertake to bear the cross, was to testify and prove his obedience to the Father; whereas there are many reasons which make it necessary for us to live constantly under the cross. Feeble as we are by nature, and prone to ascribe all perfection to our flesh, unless we receive as it were ocular demonstration of our weakness, we readily estimate our virtue above its proper worth, and doubt not that, whatever happens, it will stand unimpaired and invincible against all difficulties. Hence we indulge a stupid and empty confidence in the flesh, and then trusting to it wax proud against the Lord himself; as if our own faculties were sufficient without his grace. This arrogance cannot be better repressed than when He proves to us by experience, not only how great our weakness, but also our frailty is. Therefore, he visits us with disgrace, or poverty, or bereavement, or disease, or other afflictions. Feeling altogether unable to support them, we forthwith, in so far as regards ourselves, give way, and thus humbled learn to invoke his strength, which alone can enable us to bear up under a weight of affliction. Nay, even the holiest of men, however well aware that they stand not in their own strength, but by the grace of God, would feel too secure in their own

fortitude and constancy, were they not brought to a more thorough knowledge of themselves by the trial of the cross. This feeling gained even upon David, "In my prosperity I Said, I shall never be moved. Lord, by thy favour thou hast made my mountain to stand strong: thou didst hide thy face, and I was troubled," (Ps. 30:6, 7). He confesses that in prosperity his feelings were dulled and blunted, so that, neglecting the grace of God, on which alone he ought to have depended, he leant to himself, and promised himself perpetuity. If it so happened to this great prophet, who of us should not fear and study caution? 2018Though in tranquillity they flatter themselves with the idea of greater constancy and patience, yet, humbled by adversity, they learn the deception. Believers, I say, warned by such proofs of their diseases, make progress in humility, and, divesting themselves of a depraved confidence in the flesh, betake themselves to the grace of God, and, when they have so betaken themselves, experience the presence of the divine power, in which is ample protection.

3. This Paul teaches when he says that tribulation worketh patience, and patience experience. God having promised that he will be with believers in tribulation, they feel the truth of the promise; while supported by his hand, they endure patiently. This they could never do by their own strength. Patience, therefore, gives the saints an experimental proof that God in reality furnishes the aid which he has promised whenever there is need. Hence also their faith is confirmed, for it were very ungrateful not to expect that in future the truth of God will be, as they have already found it, firm and constant. We now see how many advantages are at once produced by the cross. Overturning the overweening opinion we form of our own virtue, and detecting the hypocrisy in which we delight, it removes our pernicious carnal confidence, teaching us, when thus humbled, to recline on God alone, so that we neither are oppressed nor despond. Then victory is followed by hope, inasmuch as the Lord, by performing what he has promised, establishes his truth in regard to the future. Were these the only reasons, it is surely plain how necessary it is for usto bear the cross. It is of no little importance to be rid of your self-love, and made fully conscious of your weakness; so impressed with a sense of your weakness as to learn to distrust yourself—to distrust yourself so as to transfer your confidence to

God, reclining on him with such heartfelt confidence as to trust in his aid, and continue invincible to the end, standing by his grace so as to perceive that he is true to his promises, and so assured of the certainty of his promises as to be strong in hope.

4. Another end which the Lord has in afflicting his people is to try their patience, and train them to obedience—not that they can yield obedience to him except in so far as he enables them; but he is pleased thus to attest and display striking proofs of the graces which he has conferred upon his saints, lest they should remain within unseen and unemployed. Accordingly, by bringing forward openly the strength and constancy of endurance with which he has provided his servants, he is said to try their patience. Hence the expressions that God tempted Abraham (Gen. 21:1, 12), and made proof of his piety by not declining to sacrifice his only son. Hence, too, Peter tells us that our faith is proved by tribulation, just as gold is tried in a furnace of fire. But who will say it is not expedient that the most excellent gift of patience which the believer has received from his God should be applied to uses by being made sure and manifest? Otherwise men would never value it according to its worth. But if God himself, to prevent the virtues which he has conferred upon believers from 2019lurking in obscurity, nay, lying useless and perishing, does aright in supplying materials for calling them forth, there is the best reason for the afflictions of the saints, since without them their patience could not exist. I say, that by the cross they are also trained to obedience, because they are thus taught to live not according to their own wish, but at the disposal of God. Indeed, did all things proceed as they wish, they would not know what it is to follow God. Seneca mentions (De Vit. Beata, cap. 15) that there was an old proverb when any one was exhorted to endure adversity, "Follow God;" thereby intimating, that men truly submitted to the yoke of God only when they gave their back and hand to his rod. But if it is most right that we should in all things prove our obedience to our heavenly Father, certainly we ought not to decline any method by which he trains us to obedience.

5. Still, however, we see not how necessary that obedience is, unless we at the same time consider how prone our carnal nature is to shake off the

yoke of God whenever it has been treated with some degree of gentleness and indulgence. It just happens to it as with refractory horses, which, if kept idle for a few days at hack and manger, become ungovernable, and no longer recognize the rider, whose command before they implicitly obeyed. And we invariably become what God complains of in the people of Israel— waxing gross and fat, we kick against him who reared and nursed us (Deut. 32:15). The kindness of God should allure us to ponder and love his goodness; but since such is our malignity, that we are invariably corrupted by his indulgence, it is more than necessary for us to be restrained by discipline from breaking forth into such petulance. Thus, lest we become emboldened by an over-abundance of wealth; lest elated with honour, we grow proud; lest inflated with other advantages of body, or mind, or fortune, we grow insolent, the Lord himself interferes as he sees to be expedient by means of the cross, subduing and curbing the arrogance of our flesh, and that in various ways, as the advantage of each requires. For as we do not all equally labour under the same disease, so we do not all need the same difficult cure. Hence we see that all are not exercised with the same kind of cross. While the heavenly Physician treats some more gently, in the case of others he employs harsher remedies, his purpose being to provide a cure for all. Still none is left free and untouched, because he knows that all, without a single exception, are diseased.

6. We may add, that our most merciful Father requires not only to prevent our weakness, but often to correct our past faults, that he may keep us in due obedience. Therefore, whenever we are afflicted we ought immediately to call to mind our past life. In this way we will find that the faults which we have committed are deserving of such castigation. And yet the exhortation to patience is not to be founded chiefly on the acknowledgment of sin. For Scripture supplies a far better consideration when it says, that in adversity "we are chastened of the Lord, that we should not be condemned with the 2020world," (1 Cor. 11:32). Therefore, in the very bitterness of tribulation we ought to recognise the kindness and mercy of our Father, since even then he ceases not to further our salvation. For he afflicts, not that he may ruin or destroy but rather that he may deliver us from the condemnation of the world. Let this thought lead us to what Scripture elsewhere teaches: "My

son, despise not the chastening of the Lord; neither be weary of his correction: For whom the Lord loveth he correcteth; even as a father the son in whom he delighteth," (Prov. 3:11, 12). When we perceive our Father's rod, is it not our part to behave as obedient docile sons rather than rebelliously imitate desperate men, who are hardened in wickedness? God dooms us to destruction, if he does not, by correction, call us back when we have fallen off from him, so that it is truly said, "If ye be without chastisement," "then are ye bastards, and not sons," (Heb. 12:8). We are most perverse then if we cannot bear him while he is manifesting his good-will to us, and the care which he takes of our salvation. Scripture states the difference between believers and unbelievers to be, that the latter, as the slaves of inveterate and deep-seated iniquity, only become worse and more obstinate under the lash; whereas the former, like free-born sons turn to repentance. Now, therefore, choose your class. But as I have already spoken of this subject, it is sufficient to have here briefly adverted to it.

7. There is singular consolation, moreover, when we are persecuted for righteousness' sake. For our thought should then be, How high the honour which God bestows upon us in distinguishing us by the special badge of his soldiers. By suffering persecution for righteousness' sake, I mean not only striving for the defence of the Gospel, but for the defence of righteousness in any way. Whether, therefore, in maintaining the truth of God against the lies of Satan, or defending the good and innocent against the injuries of the bad, we are obliged to incur the offence and hatred of the world, so as to endanger life, fortune, or honour, let us not grieve or decline so far to spend ourselves for God; let us not think ourselves wretched in those things in which he with his own lips has pronounced us blessed (Mt. 5:10). Poverty, indeed considered in itself, is misery; so are exile, contempt, imprisonment, ignominy: in fine, death itself is the last of all calamities. But when the favour of God breathes upon is, there is none of these things which may not turn out to our happiness. Let us then be contented with the testimony of Christ rather than with the false estimate of the flesh, and then, after the example of the Apostles, we will rejoice in being "counted worthy to suffer shame for his name," (Acts 5:41). For why? If, while conscious of our innocence, we are deprived of our substance by the wickedness of man, we

are, no doubt, humanly speaking, reduced to poverty; but in truth our riches in heaven are increased: if driven from our homes we have a more welcome reception into the family of God; if vexed and despised, we are more firmly rooted in Christ; if stigmatised by disgrace and ignominy, we have a higher place in the kingdom of God; and if we are slain, entrance is thereby given us to eternal life. The Lord having set such a price upon us, let us be ashamed to estimate ourselves at less than the shadowy and evanescent allurements of the present life.

8. Since by these, and similar considerations, Scripture abundantly solaces us for the ignominy or calamities which we endure in defence of righteousness, we are very ungrateful if we do not willingly and cheerfully receive them at the hand of the Lord, especially since this form of the cross is the most appropriate to believers, being that by which Christ desires to be glorified in us, as Peter also declares (1 Pet. 4:11, 14). But as to ingenuous natures, it is more bitter to suffer disgrace than a hundred deaths, Paul expressly reminds us that not only persecution, but also disgrace awaits us, "because we trust in the living God," (1 Tim. 4:10). So in another passage he bids us, after his example, walk "by evil report and good report," (2 Cor. 6:8). The cheerfulness required, however, does not imply a total insensibility to pain. The saints could show no patience under the cross if they were not both tortured with pain and grievously molested. Were there no hardship in poverty, no pain in disease, no sting in ignominy, no fear in death, where would be the fortitude and moderation in enduring them? But while every one of these, by its inherent bitterness, naturally vexes the mind, the believer in this displays his fortitude, that though fully sensible of the bitterness and labouring grievously, he still withstands and struggles boldly; in this displays his patience, that though sharply stung, he is however curbed by the fear of God from breaking forth into any excess; in this displays his alacrity, that though pressed with sorrow and sadness, he rests satisfied with spiritual consolation from God.

9. This conflict which believers maintain against the natural feeling of pain, while they study moderation and patience, Paul elegantly describes in these words: "We are troubled on every side, yet not distressed; we are

perplexed, but not in despair; persecuted, but not forsaken; cast down, but not destroyed," (2 Cor. 4:8, 9). You see that to bear the cross patiently is not to have your feelings altogether blunted, and to be absolutely insensible to pain, according to the absurd description which the Stoics of old gave of their hero as one who, divested of humanity, was affected in the same way by adversity and prosperity, grief and joy; or rather, like a stone, was not affected by anything. And what did they gain by that sublime wisdom? they exhibited a shadow of patience, which never did, and never can, exist among men. Nay, rather by aiming at a too exact and rigid patience, they banished it altogether from human life. Now also we have among Christians a new kind of Stoics, who hold it vicious not only to groan and weep, but even to be sad and anxious. These paradoxes are usually started by indolent men who, employing themselves more in speculation than in action, can do nothing else for us than beget such paradoxes. But we have nothing to do with 2022that iron philosophy which our Lord and Master condemned— not only in word, but also by his own example. For he both grieved and shed tears for his own and others' woes. Nor did he teach his disciples differently: "Ye shall weep and lament, but the world shall rejoice," (John 16:20). And lest any one should regard this as vicious, he expressly declares, "Blessed are they that mourn," (Mt. 5:4). And no wonder. If all tears are condemned, what shall we think of our Lord himself, whose "sweat was as it were great drops of blood falling down to the ground?" (Luke 22:44; Mt. 26:38). If every kind of fear is a mark of unbelief, what place shall we assign to the dread which, it is said, in no slight degree amazed him; if all sadness is condemned, how shall we justify him when he confesses, "My soul is exceeding sorrowful, even unto death?"

10. I wished to make these observations to keep pious minds from despair, lest, from feeling it impossible to divest themselves of the natural feeling of grief, they might altogether abandon the study of patience. This must necessarily be the result with those who convert patience into stupor, and a brave and firm man into a block. Scripture gives saints the praise of endurance when, though afflicted by the hardships they endure, they are not crushed; though they feel bitterly, they are at the same time filled with spiritual joy; though pressed with anxiety, breathe exhilarated by the consolation

of God. Still there is a certain degree of repugnance in their hearts, because natural sense shuns and dreads what is adverse to it, while pious affection, even through these difficulties, tries to obey the divine will. This repugnance the Lord expressed when he thus addressed Peter: "Verily, verily, I say unto thee, When thou wast young, thou girdedst thyself and walkedst whither thou wouldst; but when thou shalt be old, thou shalt stretch forth thy hands, and another shall gird thee; and carry thee whither thou wouldest not," (John 21:18). It is not probable, indeed, that when it became necessary to glorify God by death he was driven to it unwilling and resisting; had it been so, little praise would have been due to his martyrdom. But though he obeyed the divine ordination with the greatest alacrity of heart, yet, as he had not divested himself of humanity, he was distracted by a double will. When he thought of the bloody death which he was to die, struck with horror, he would willingly have avoided it: on the other hand, when he considered that it was God who called him to it, his fear was vanquished and suppressed, and he met death cheerfully. It must therefore be our study, if we would be disciples of Christ, to imbue our minds with such reverence and obedience to God as may tame and subjugate all affections contrary to his appointment. In this way, whatever be the kind of cross to which we are subjected, we shall in the greatest straits firmly maintain our patience. Adversity will have its bitterness, and sting us. When afflicted with disease, we shall groan and be disquieted, and long for health; pressed with 2023poverty, we shall feel the stings of anxiety and sadness, feel the pain of ignominy, contempt, and injury, and pay the tears due to nature at the death of our friends: but our conclusion will always be, The Lord so willed it, therefore let us follow his will. Nay, amid the pungency of grief, among groans and tears this thought will necessarily suggest itself and incline us cheerfully to endure the things for which we are so afflicted.

11. But since the chief reason for enduring the cross has been derived from a consideration of the divine will, we must in few words explain wherein lies the difference between philosophical and Christian patience. Indeed, very few of the philosophers advanced so far as to perceive that the hand of God tries us by means of affliction, and that we ought in this matter to obey God. The only reason which they adduce is, that so it must be. But is

not this just to say, that we must yield to God, because it is in vain to contend against him? For if we obey God only because it is necessary, provided we can escape, we shall cease to obey him. But what Scripture calls us to consider in the will of God is very different, namely, first justice and equity, and then a regard to our own salvation. Hence Christian exhortations to patience are of this nature, Whether poverty, or exile, or imprisonment, or contumely, or disease, or bereavement, or any such evil affects us, we must think that none of them happens except by the will and providence of God; moreover, that every thing he does is in the most perfect order. What! do not our numberless daily faults deserve to be chastised, more severely, and with a heavier rod than his mercy lays upon us? Is it not most right that our flesh should be subdued, and be, as it were, accustomed to the yoke, so as not to rage and wanton as it lists? Are not the justice and the truth of God worthy of our suffering on their account? But if the equity of God is undoubtedly displayed in affliction, we cannot murmur or struggle against them without iniquity. We no longer hear the frigid cant, Yield, because it is necessary; but a living and energetic precept, Obey, because it is unlawful to resist; bear patiently, because impatience is rebellion against the justice of God. Then as that only seems to us attractive which we perceive to be for our own safety and advantage, here also our heavenly Father consoles us, by the assurance, that in the very cross with which he afflicts us he provides for our salvation. But if it is clear that tribulations are salutary to us, why should we not receive them with calm and grateful minds? In bearing them patiently we are not submitting to necessity but resting satisfied with our own good. The effect of these thoughts is, that to whatever extent our minds are contracted by the bitterness which we naturally feel under the cross, to the same extent will they be expanded with spiritual joy. Hence arises thanksgiving, which cannot exist unless joy be felt. But if the praise of the Lord and thanksgiving can emanate only from a cheerful and gladdened breasts and there is nothing which ought to interrupt these feelings in us, it is clear how necessary it is to temper the bitterness of the cross with spiritual joy.

CHAPTER 9: OF MEDITATING ON THE FUTURE LIFE

1. Whatever be the kind of tribulation with which we are afflicted, we should always consider the end of it to be, that we may be trained to despise the present, and thereby stimulated to aspire to the future life. For since God well knows how strongly we are inclined by nature to a slavish love of this world, in order to prevent us from clinging too strongly to it, he employs the fittest reason for calling us back, and shaking off our lethargy. Every one of us, indeed, would be thought to aspire and aim at heavenly immortality during the whole course of his life. For we would be ashamed in no respect to excel the lower animals; whose condition would not be at all inferior to ours, had we not a hope of immortality beyond the grave. But when you attend to the plans, wishes, and actions of each, you see nothing in them but the earth. Hence our stupidity; our minds being dazzled with the glare of wealth, power, and honours, that they can see no farther. The heart also, engrossed with avarice, ambition, and lust, is weighed down and cannot rise above them. In short, the whole soul, ensnared by the allurements of the flesh, seeks its happiness on the earth. To meet this disease, the Lord makes his people sensible of the vanity of the present life, by a constant proof of its miseries. Thus, that they may not promise themselves deep and lasting peace in it, he often allows them to be assailed by war, tumult, or rapine, or to be disturbed by other injuries. That they may not long with too much eagerness after fleeting and fading riches, or rest in those which they already possess, he reduces them to want, or, at least, restricts them to a moderate allowance, at one time by exile, at another by sterility, at another by fire, or by other means. That they may not indulge too complacently in the advantages of married life, he either vexes them by the misconduct of their partners, or humbles them by the wickedness of their children, or afflicts them by bereavement. But if in all these he is indulgent to them, lest they should either swell with vain-glory, or be elated with confidence, by diseases and dangers he sets palpably before them how unstable and evanescent are all the advantages competent to mortals. We duly profit by the discipline of the cross, when we learn that this life, estimated in itself, is restless, troubled, in numberless ways wretched, and plainly in no respect

happy; that what are estimated its blessings are uncertain, fleeting, vain, and vitiated by a great admixture of evil. From this we conclude, that all we have to seek or hope for here is contest; that when we think of the crown we must raise our eyes to heaven. For we must hold, that our mind never rises seriously to desire and aspire after the future, until it has learned to despise the present life.

2. For there is no medium between the two things: the earth must either be worthless in our estimation, or keep us enslaved by an intemperate love of it. Therefore, if we have any regard to eternity, we must carefully strive to disencumber ourselves of these fetters. Moreover, since the present life has many enticements to allure us, and great semblance of delight, grace, and sweetness to soothe us, it is of great consequence to us to be now and then called off from its fascinations. For what, pray, would happen, if we here enjoyed an uninterrupted course of honour and felicity, when even the constant stimulus of affliction cannot arouse us to a due sense of our misery? That human life is like smoke or a shadow, is not only known to the learned; there is not a more trite proverb among the vulgar. Considering it a fact most useful to be known, they have recommended it in many well-known expressions. Still there is no fact which we ponder less carefully, or less frequently remember. For we form all our plans just as if we had fixed our immortality on the earth. If we see a funeral, or walk among graves, as the image of death is then present to the eye, I admit we philosophise admirably on the vanity of life. We do not indeed always do so, for those things often have no effect upon us at all. But, at the best, our philosophy is momentary. It vanishes as soon as we turn our back, and leaves not the vestige of remembrance behind; in short, it passes away, just like the applause of a theatre at some pleasant spectacle. Forgetful not only of death, but also of mortality itself, as if no rumour of it had ever reached us, we indulge in supine security as expecting a terrestrial immortality. Meanwhile, if any one breaks in with the proverb, that man is the creature of a day, we indeed acknowledge its truth, but, so far from giving heed to it, the thought of perpetuity still keeps hold of our minds. Who then can deny that it is of the highest importance to us all, I say not, to be admonished by words, but convinced by all possible experience of the miserable condition of our

earthly life; since even when convinced we scarcely cease to gaze upon it with vicious, stupid admiration, as if it contained within itself the sum of all that is good? But if God finds it necessary so to train us, it must be our duty to listen to him when he calls, and shakes us from our torpor, that we may hasten to despise the world, and aspire with our whole heart to the future life.

3. Still the contempt which believers should train themselves to feel for the present life, must not be of a kind to beget hatred of it or ingratitude to God. This life, though abounding in all kinds of wretchedness, is justly classed among divine blessings which are not to be despised. Wherefore, if we do not recognize the kindness of God in it, we are chargeable with no little ingratitude towards him. To believers, especially, it ought to be a proof of divine benevolence, since it is wholly destined to promote their salvation. Before openly exhibiting the inheritance of eternal glory, God is pleased to manifest himself to us as a Father by minor proofs—viz. the blessings which he daily bestows upon us. Therefore, while this life serves to acquaint us with the goodness of God, shall we disdain it as if it did not contain one particle of good? We ought, therefore, to feel and be affected towards it in such a manner as to place it among those gifts of the divine benignity which are by no means to be despised. Were there no proofs in Scripture (they are most numerous and clear), yet nature herself exhorts us to return thanks to God for having brought us forth into light, granted us the use of it, and bestowed upon us all the means necessary for its preservation. And there is a much higher reason when we reflect that here we are in a manner prepared for the glory of the heavenly kingdom. For the Lord hath ordained, that those who are ultimately to be crowned in heaven must maintain a previous warfare on the earth, that they may not triumph before they have overcome the difficulties of war, and obtained the victory. Another reason is, that we here begin to experience in various ways a foretaste of the divine benignity, in 2028order that our hope and desire may be whetted for its full manifestation. When once we have concluded that our earthly life is a gift of the divine mercy, of which, agreeably to our obligation, it behoves us to have a grateful remembrance, we shall then properly descend to consider its most wretched condition, and thus escape from that excessive fondness for it, to

which, as I have said, we are naturally prone.

4. In proportion as this improper love diminishes, our desire of a better life should increase. I confess, indeed, that a most accurate opinion was formed by those who thought, that the best thing was not to be born, the next best to die early. For, being destitute of the light of God and of true religion, what could they see in it that was not of dire and evil omen? Nor was it unreasonable for those who felt sorrow and shed tears at the birth of their kindred, to keep holiday at their deaths. But this they did without profit; because, devoid of the true doctrine of faith, they saw not how that which in itself is neither happy nor desirable turns to the advantage of the righteous: and hence their opinion issued in despair. Let believers, then, in forming an estimate of this mortal life, and perceiving that in itself it is nothing but misery, make it their aim to exert themselves with greater alacrity, and less hinderance, in aspiring to the future and eternal life. When we contrast the two, the former may not only be securely neglected, but, in comparison of the latter, be disdained and contemned. If heaven is our country, what can the earth be but a place of exile? If departure from the world is entrance into life, what is the world but a sepulchre, and what is residence in it but immersion in death? If to be freed from the body is to gain full possession of freedom, what is the body but a prison? If it is the very summit of happiness to enjoy the presence of God, is it not miserable to want it? But "whilst we are at home in the body, we are absent from the Lord," (2 Cor. 5:6). Thus when the earthly is compared with the heavenly life, it may undoubtedly be despised and trampled under foot. We ought never, indeed, to regard it with hatred, except in so far as it keeps us subject to sin; and even this hatred ought not to be directed against life itself. At all events, we must stand so affected towards it in regard to weariness or hatred as, while longing for its termination, to be ready at the Lord's will to continue in it, keeping far from everything like murmuring and impatience. For it is as if the Lord had assigned us a post, which we must maintain till he recalls us. Paul, indeed, laments his condition, in being still bound with the fetters of the body, and sighs earnestly for redemption (Rom. 7:24); nevertheless, he declared that, in obedience to the command of Gods he was prepared for both courses, because he acknowledges it as his duty to God to glorify

his name whether by life or by death, while it belongs to God to deter-
mine what is most conducive to His glory (Phil. 1:20-24). Wherefore, if it
becomes us to live and die to the Lord, let us leave the period of our life
and death at his disposal. Still let us ardently long for death, and constantly
meditate upon it, and in comparison with future immortality, let us despise
life, and, on account of the bondage of sin, long to renounce it whenever it
shall so please the Lord.

5. But, most strange to say, many who boast of being Christians, instead of
thus longing for death, are so afraid of it that they tremble at the very mention of it as a thing ominous and dreadful. We cannot wonder, indeed, that
our natural feelings should be somewhat shocked at the mention of our
dissolution. But it is altogether intolerable that the light of piety should not
be so powerful in a Christian breast as with greater consolation to overcome
and suppress that fear. For if we reflect that this our tabernacle, unstable,
defective, corruptible, fading, pining, and putrid, is dissolved, in order that it
may forthwith be renewed in sure, perfect, incorruptible, in fine, in heavenly
glory, will not faith compel us eagerly to desire what nature dreads? If we
reflect that by death we are recalled from exile to inhabit our native country, a heavenly country, shall this give us no comfort? But everything longs
for permanent existence. I admit this, and therefore contend that we ought
to look to future immortality, where we may obtain that fixed condition
which nowhere appears on the earth. For Paul admirably enjoins believers
to hasten cheerfully to death, not because they "would be unclothed, but
clothed upon," (2 Cor. 5:2). Shall the lower animals, and inanimate creatures
themselves even wood and stone, as conscious of their present vanity, long
for the final resurrection, that they may with the sons of God be delivered
from vanity (Rom. 8:19); and shall we, endued with the light of intellect,
and more than intellect, enlightened by the Spirit of God, when our essence
is in question, rise no higher than the corruption of this earth? But it is not
my purpose, nor is this the place, to plead against this great perverseness. At
the outset, I declared that I had no wish to engage in a diffuse discussion of
common-places. My advice to those whose minds are thus timid is to read
the short treatise of Cyprian De Mortalitate, unless it be more accordant
with their deserts to send them to the philosophers, that by inspecting what

they say on the contempt of death, they may begin to blush. This, however let us hold as fixed, that no man has made much progress in the school of Christ who does not look forward with joy to the day of death and final resurrection (2 Tim. 4:18; Tit. 2:13) for Paul distinguishes all believers by this mark; and the usual course of Scripture is to direct us thither whenever it would furnish us with an argument for substantial joy. "Look up," says our Lord, "and lift up your heads: for your redemption draweth nigh," (Luke 21:28). Is it reasonable, I ask, that what he intended to have a powerful effect in stirring us up to alacrity and exultation should produce nothing but sadness and consternation? If it is so, why do we still glory in him as our Master? Therefore, let us come to a sounder mind, and how repugnant so ever the blind and stupid longing of the flesh may be, let us doubt not to desire the advent of the Lord not in wish only, but with earnest sighs, as the most propitious of all events. He will come as a Redeemer to deliver us from an immense abyss of evil and misery, and lead us to the blessed inheritance of his life and glory.

6. Thus, indeed, it is; the whole body of the faithful, so long as they live on the earth, must be like sheep for the slaughter, in order that they may be conformed to Christ their head (Rom. 8:36). Most deplorable, therefore, would their situation be did they not, by raising their mind to heaven, become superior to all that is in the world, and rise above the present aspect of affairs (1 Cor. 15:19). On the other hand, when once they have raised their head above all earthly objects, though they see the wicked flourishing in wealth and honour, and enjoying profound peace, indulging in luxury and splendour, and revelling in all kinds of delights, though they should moreover be wickedly assailed by them, suffer insult from their pride, be robbed by their avarice, or assailed by any other passion, they will have no difficulty in bearing up under these evils. They will turn their eye to that day (Isaiah 25:8; Rev. 7:17), on which the Lord will receive his faithful servants, wipe away all tears from their eyes, clothe them in a robe of glory and joy, feed them with the ineffable sweetness of his pleasures, exalt them to share with him in his greatness; in fine, admit them to a participation in his happiness. But the wicked who may have flourished on the earth, he will cast forth in extreme ignominy, will change their delights into torments, their laughter

and joy into wailing and gnashing of teeth, their peace into the gnawing of conscience, and punish their luxury with unquenchable fire. He will also place their necks under the feet of the godly, whose patience they abused. For, as Paul declares, "it is a righteous thing with God to recompense tribulation to them that trouble you; and to you who are troubled rest with us, when the Lord Jesus shall be revealed from heaven," (2 Thess. 1:6, 7). This, indeed, is our only consolation; deprived of it, we must either give way to despondency, or resort to our destruction to the vain solace of the world. The Psalmist confesses, "My feet were almost gone: my steps had well nigh slipt: for I was envious at the foolish when I saw the prosperity of the wicked," (Psalm 73:3, 4); and he found no resting-place until he entered the sanctuary, and considered the latter end of the righteous and the wicked. To conclude in one word, the cross of Christ then only triumphs in the breasts of believers over the devil and the flesh, sin and sinners, when their eyes are directed to the power of his resurrection.

MARTIN LUTHER'S COMMENTARY ON GALATIANS 3

TOP TEN THEOLOGIANS

CHAPTER III

Verse 3. Are ye so foolish? having begun in the Spirit, are ye now made perfect by the flesh?

Paul now begins to warn the Galatians against a twofold danger. The first danger is: "Are ye so foolish, that after ye have begun in the Spirit, ye would now end in the flesh?"

"Flesh" stands for the righteousness of reason which seeks justification by the accomplishment of the Law. I am told that I began in the spirit under the papacy, but am ending up in the flesh because I got married. As though single life were a spiritual life, and married life a carnal life. They are silly. All the duties of a Christian husband, e.g., to love his wife, to bring up his children, to govern his family, etc., are the very fruits of the Spirit.

The righteousness of the Law which Paul also terms the righteousness of the flesh is so far from justifying a person that those who once had the Holy Spirit and lost Him, end up in the Law to their complete destruction.

Verse 4. Have ye suffered so many things in vain?

The other danger against which the Apostle warns the Galatians is this: "Have ye suffered so many things in vain?" Paul wants to say: "Consider not only the good start you had and lost, but consider also the many things you have suffered for the sake of the Gospel and for the name of Christ. You have suffered the loss of your possessions, you have borne reproaches, you have passed through many dangers of body and life. You endured much for the name of Christ and you endured it faithfully. But now you have lost everything, the Gospel, faith, and the spiritual benefit of your sufferings for Christ's sake. What a miserable thing to endure so many afflictions for nothing."

Verse 4. If it be yet in vain.

The Apostle adds the afterthought: "If it be yet in vain. I do not despair of all hope for you. But if you continue to look to the Law for righteousness, I think you should be told that all your past true worship of God and all the afflictions that you have endured for Christ's sake are going to help you not at all. I do not mean to discourage you altogether. I do hope you will repent and amend."

Verse 5. He therefore that ministereth to you the Spirit, and worketh miracles among you, doeth he it by the works of the law, or by the hearing of faith?

This argument based on the experience of the Galatians, pleased the Apostle so well that he returns to it after he had warned them against their twofold danger. "You have not only received the Spirit by the preaching of the Gospel, but by the same Gospel you were enabled to do things." "What things?" we ask. Miracles. At least the Galatians had manifested the striking fruits of faith which true disciples of the Gospel manifested in those days. On one occasion the Apostle wrote: "The kingdom of God is not in word, but in power." This "power" revealed itself not only in readiness of speech, but in demonstrations of the supernatural ability of the Holy Spirit.

When the Gospel is preached unto faith, hope, love, and patience, God gives His wonder-working Spirit. Paul reminds the Galatians of this. "God had not only brought you to faith by my preaching. He had also sanctified you to bring forth the fruits of faith. And one of the fruits of your faith was that you loved me so devotedly that you were willing to pluck out your eyes for me." To love a fellow-man so devotedly as to be ready to bestow upon him money, goods, eyes in order to secure his salvation, such love is the fruit of the Holy Spirit.

"These products of the Spirit you enjoyed before the false apostles misled you," the Apostle reminds the Galatians. "But you haven't manifested any of these fruits under the regime of the Law. How does it come that you do not grow the same fruits now? You no longer teach truly; you do not believe boldly; you do not live well; you do not work hard; you do not bear things patiently. Who has spoiled you that you no longer love me; that you are not now ready to pluck out your eyes for me? What has happened to cool your personal interest in me?"

The same thing happened to me. When I began to proclaim the Gospel, there were many, very many who were delighted with our doctrine and had a good opinion of us. And now? Now they have succeeded in making us so odious to those who formerly loved us that they now hate us like poison.

Paul argues: "Your experience ought to teach you that the fruits of love do not grow on the stump of the Law. You had not virtue prior to the preaching of the Gospel and you have no virtues now under the regime of the false apostles."

We, too, may say to those who misname themselves "evangelical" and flout their new-found liberty: Have you put down the tyranny of the Pope and obtained liberty in Christ through the Anabaptists and other fanatics? Or have you obtained your freedom from us who preach faith in Christ Jesus? If there is any honesty left in them they will have to confess that their freedom dates from the preaching of the Gospel.

Verse 6. Even as Abraham believed God, and it was accounted to him for righteousness.

The Apostle next adduces the example of Abraham and reviews the testimony of the Scriptures concerning faith. The first passage is taken from Genesis 15:6: "And he believed in the Lord; and he counted it to him for righteousness." The Apostle makes the most of this passage. Abraham may have enjoyed a good standing with men for his upright life, but not with God. In the sight of God, Abraham was a condemned sinner. That he was justified before God was not due to his own exertions, but due to his faith. The Scriptures expressly state: "Abraham believed in the Lord; and he counted it to him for righteousness."

Paul places the emphasis upon the two words: Abraham believed. Faith in God constitutes the highest worship, the prime duty, the first obedience, and the foremost sacrifice. Without faith God forfeits His glory, wisdom, truth, and mercy in us. The first duty of man is to believe in God and to honor Him with his faith. Faith is truly the height of wisdom, the right kind of righteousness, the only real religion. This will give us an idea of the excellence of faith.

To believe in God as Abraham did is to be right with God because faith honors God. Faith says to God: "I believe what you say."

When we pay attention to reason, God seems to propose impossible matters in the Christian Creed. To reason it seems absurd that Christ should offer His body and blood in the Lord's Supper; that Baptism should be the washing of regeneration; that the dead shall rise; that Christ the Son of God was conceived in the womb of the Virgin Mary, etc. Reason shouts that all this is preposterous. Are you surprised that reason thinks little of faith? Reason thinks it ludicrous that faith should be the foremost service any person can render unto God.

Let your faith supplant reason. Abraham mastered reason by faith in the Word of God. Not as though reason ever yields meekly. It put up a fight against the faith of Abraham. Reason protested that it was absurd to think that Sarah who was ninety years old and barren by nature, should give birth to a son. But faith won the victory and routed reason, that ugly beast and enemy of God. Everyone who by faith slays reason, the world's biggest monster, renders God a real service, a better service than the religions of all races and all the drudgery of meritorious monks can render.

Men fast, pray, watch, suffer. They intend to appease the wrath of God and to deserve God's grace by their exertions. But there is no glory in it for God, because by their exertions these workers pronounce God an unmerciful slave driver, an unfaithful and angry Judge. They despise God, make a liar out of Him, snub Christ and all His benefits; in short they pull God from His throne and perch themselves on it.

Faith truly honors God. And because faith honors God, God counts faith for righteousness.

Christian righteousness is the confidence of the heart in God through Christ Jesus. Such confidence is accounted righteousness for Christ's sake. Two things make for Christian righteousness: Faith in Christ, which is a gift of God; and God's acceptance of this imperfect faith of ours for perfect righteousness. Because of my faith in Christ, God overlooks my distrust, the unwillingness of my spirit, my many other sins. Because the shadow of Christ's wing covers me I have no fear that God will cover all my sins and take my imperfections for perfect righteousness.

God "winks" at my sins and covers them up. God says: "Because you believe in My Son I will forgive your sins until death shall deliver you from the body of sin."

Learn to understand the constitution of your Christian righteousness. Faith is weak, but it means enough to God that He will not lay sin to our charge. He will not punish nor condemn us for it. He will forgive our sins as though they amount to nothing at all. He will do it not because we are worthy of such mercy. He will do it for Jesus' sake in whom we believe.

Paradoxically, a Christian is both right and wrong, holy and profane, an enemy of God and a child of God. These contradictions no person can harmonize who does not understand the true way of salvation. Under the papacy we were told to toil until the feeling of guilt had left us. But the authors of this deranged idea were frequently driven to despair in the hour of death. It would have happened to me, if Christ had not mercifully delivered me from this error.

We comfort the afflicted sinner in this manner: Brother, you can never be perfect in this life, but you can be holy. He will say: "How can I be holy when I feel my sins?" I answer: You feel sin? That is a good sign. To realize that one is ill is a step, and a very necessary step, toward recovery. "But how will I get rid of my sin?" he will ask. I answer: See the heavenly Physician, Christ, who heals the broken-hearted. Do not consult that Quackdoctor, Reason. Believe in Christ and your sins will be pardoned. His righteousness will become your righteousness, and your sins will become His sins.

On one occasion Jesus said to His disciples: "The Father loveth you." Why? Not because the disciples were Pharisees, or circumcised, or particularly attentive to the Law. Jesus said: "The Father loveth you, because ye have loved me, and have believed that I came out from God. It pleased you to know that the Father sent me into the world. And because you believed it the Father loves you." On another occasion Jesus called His disciples evil and commanded them to ask for forgiveness.

A Christian is beloved of God and a sinner. How can these two contradictions be harmonized: I am a sinner and deserve God's wrath and punishment, and yet the Father loves me? Christ alone can harmonize these contradictions. He is the Mediator.

Do you now see how faith justifies without works? Sin lingers in us, and God hates sin. A transfusion of righteousness therefore becomes vitally necessary. This transfusion of righteousness we obtain from Christ because we believe in Him.

Verse 7. Know ye therefore that they which are of faith, the same are the children of Abraham.

This is the main point of Paul's argument against the Jews: The children of Abraham are those who believe and not those who are born of Abraham's flesh and blood. This point Paul drives home with all his might because the Jews attached saving value to the genealogical fact: "We are the seed and children of Abraham."

Let us begin with Abraham and learn how this friend of God was justified and saved. Not because he left his country, his relatives, his father's house; not because he was circumcised; not because he stood ready to sacrifice his own son Isaac in whom he had the promise of posterity. Abraham was justified because he believed. Paul's argumentation runs like this: "Since this is the unmistakable testimony of Holy Writ, why do you take your stand upon circumcision and the Law? Was not Abraham, your father, of whom you make so much, justified and saved without circumcision and the Law by faith alone?" Paul therefore concludes: "They which are of faith, the same are the children of Abraham."

Abraham was the father of the faithful. In order to be a child of the believing Abraham you must believe as he did. Otherwise you are merely the physical offspring of the procreating Abraham, i.e., you were conceived and born in sin unto wrath and condemnation.

Ishmael and Isaac were both the natural children of Abraham. By rights Ishmael should have enjoyed the prerogatives of the firstborn, if physical generation had any special value. Nevertheless he was left out in the cold while Isaac was called. This goes to prove that the children of faith are the real children of Abraham.

Some find fault with Paul for applying the term "faith" in Genesis 15:6 to Christ. They think Paul's use of the term too wide and general. They think its meaning should be restricted to the context. They claim Abraham's faith had no more in it than a belief in the promise of God that he should have seed.

We reply: Faith presupposes the assurance of God's mercy. This assurance takes in the confidence that our sins are forgiven for Christ's sake. Never will the conscience trust in God unless it can be sure of God's mercy and promises in Christ. Now all the promises of God lead back to the first promise concerning Christ: "And I will put enmity between thee and the woman, and between thy seed and her seed; it shall bruise thy head, and thou shalt bruise his heel." The faith of the fathers in the Old Testament era, and our faith in the New Testament are one and the same faith in Christ Jesus, although times and conditions may differ. Peter acknowledged this in the words: "Which neither our fathers nor we were able to bear? But we believe that through the grace of the Lord Jesus Christ we shall be saved, even as they" (Acts 15: 10, 11). And Paul writes: "And did all drink the spiritual drink; for they drank of that spiritual Rock that followed them: and that Rock was Christ" (I Cor. 10:4). And Christ Himself declared: "Your father Abraham rejoiced to see my day: and he saw it and was glad" (John 8:56). The faith of the fathers was directed at the Christ who was to come, while ours rests in the Christ who has come. Time does not change the object of true faith, or the Holy Spirit. There has always been and always will be one mind, one impression, one faith concerning Christ among true believers whether they live in times past, now, or in times to come. We too believe in the Christ to come as the fathers did in the Old Testament, for we look for Christ to come again on the last day to judge the quick and the dead.

Verse 7. Know ye therefore that they which are of faith, the same are the children of Abraham.

Paul is saying: "You know from the example of Abraham and from the plain testimony of the Scriptures that they are the children of Abraham, who have faith in Christ, regardless of their nationality, regardless of the Law, regardless of works, regardless of their parentage. The promise was made unto Abraham, 'Thou shalt be a father of many nations'; again, 'And in thee shall all families of the earth be blessed.'" To prevent the Jews from misinterpreting the word "nations," the Scriptures are careful to say "many nations." The true children of Abraham are the believers in Christ from all nations.

Verse 8. And the Scripture, foreseeing that God would justify the heathen through faith.

"Your boasting does not get you anywhere," says Paul to the Galatians, "because the Sacred Scriptures foresaw and foretold long before the Law was ever given, that the heathen should be justified by the blessed 'seed' of Abraham and not by the Law. This promise was made four hundred and thirty years before the Law was given. Because the Law was given so many years after Abraham, it could not abolish the promised blessing." This argument is strong because it is based on the exact factor of time. "Why should you boast of the Law, my Galatians, when the Law came four hundred and thirty years after the promise?"

The false apostles glorified the Law and despised the promise made unto Abraham, although it antedated the Law by many years. It was after Abraham was accounted righteous because of his faith that the Scriptures first make mention of circumcision. "The Scriptures," says Paul, "meant to forestall your infatuation for the righteousness of the Law by installing the righteousness of faith before circumcision and the Law ever were ordained."

Verse 8. Preached before the gospel unto Abraham, saying, In thee shall all nations be blessed.

The Jews misconstrue this passage. They want the term "to bless" to mean "to praise." They want the passage to read: In thee shall all the nations of the earth be praised. But this is a perversion of the words of Holy Writ. With the words "Abraham believed" Paul describes a spiritual Abraham, renewed by faith and regenerated by the Holy Ghost, that he should be the spiritual father of many nations. In that way all the Gentiles could be given to him for an inheritance.

The Scriptures ascribe no righteousness to Abraham except through faith. The Scriptures speak of Abraham as he stands before God, a man justified by faith. Because of his faith God extends to him the promise: "In thee shall all nations be blessed."

Verse 9. So then they which be of faith are blessed with faithful Abraham.

The emphasis lies on the words "with faithful Abraham." Paul distinguishes between Abraham and Abraham. There is a working and there is a believing Abraham. With the working Abraham we have nothing to do. Let the Jews glory in the generating Abraham; we glory in the believing Abraham of whom the Scriptures say that he received the blessing of righteousness by faith, not only for himself but for all who believe as he did. The world was promised to Abraham because he believed. The whole world is blessed if it believes as Abraham believed.

The blessing is the promise of the Gospel. That all nations are to be blessed means that all nations are to hear the Gospel. All nations are to be declared righteous before God through faith in Christ Jesus. To bless simply means to spread abroad the knowledge of Christ's salvation. This is the office of the New Testament Church which distributes the promised blessing by preaching the Gospel, by administering the sacraments, by comforting the broken-hearted, in short, by dispensing the benefits of Christ.

The Jews exhibited a working Abraham. The Pope exhibits a working Christ, or an exemplary Christ. The Pope quotes Christ's saying recorded in John 13:15, "I have given you an example, that ye should do as I have done to you." We do not deny that Christians ought to imitate the example of Christ; but mere imitation will not satisfy God. And bear in mind that Paul is not now discussing the example of Christ, but the salvation of Christ.

That Abraham submitted to circumcision at the command of God, that he was endowed with excellent virtues, that he obeyed God in all things, was certainly admirable of him. To follow the example of Christ, to love one's neighbor, to do good to them that persecute you, to pray for one's enemies, patiently to bear the ingratitude of those who return evil for good, is certainly praiseworthy. But praiseworthy or not, such virtues do not acquit us before God. It takes more than that to make us righteous before God. We need Christ Himself, not His example, to save us. We need a redeeming, not an exemplary Christ, to save us. Paul is here speaking of the redeeming Christ and the believing Abraham, not of the model Christ or the sweating Abraham.

The believing Abraham is not to lie buried in the grave. He is to be dusted off and brought out before the world. He is to be praised to the sky for his faith. Heaven and earth ought to know about him and about his faith in Christ. The working Abraham ought to look pretty small next to the believing Abraham.

Paul's words contain the implication of contrast. When he quotes Scripture to the effect that all nations that share the faith of faithful Abraham are to be blessed, Paul means to imply the contrast that all nations are accursed without faith in Christ.

Verse 10. For as many as are of the works of the law are under the curse.

The curse of God is like a flood that swallows everything that is not of faith. To avoid the curse we must hold on to the promise of the blessing in Christ.

The reader is reminded that all this has no bearing upon civil laws, customs, or political matters. Civil laws and ordinances have their place and purpose. Let every government enact the best possible laws. But civil righteousness will never deliver a person from the condemnation of God's Law.

I have good reason for calling your attention to this. People easily mistake civil righteousness for spiritual righteousness. In civil life we must, of course, pay attention to laws and deeds, but in the spiritual life we must not think to be justified by laws and works, but always keep in mind the promise and blessing of Christ, our only Savior.

According to Paul everything that is not of faith is sin. When our opponents hear us repeat this statement of Paul, they make it appear as if we taught that governments should not be honored, as if we favored rebellion against the constituted authorities, as if we condemned all laws. Our opponents do us a great wrong, for we make a clear-cut distinction between civil and spiritual affairs.

Governmental laws and ordinances are blessings of God for this life only. As for everlasting life, temporal blessings are not good enough. Unbelievers enjoy more temporal blessings than the Christians. Civil or legal righteousness may be good enough for this life but not for the life hereafter. Otherwise the infidels would be nearer heaven than the Christians, for infidels often excel in civil righteousness.

Verse 10. For it is written, Cursed is every one that continueth not in all things which are written in the book of the law to do them.

Paul goes on to prove from this quotation out of the Book of Deuteronomy that all men who are under the Law are under the sentence of sin, of the wrath of God, and of everlasting death. Paul produces his proof in a roundabout way. He turns the negative statement, "Cursed is every one that continueth not in all things which are written in the book of the law to do them," into a positive statement, "As many as are of the works of the law are under the curse." These two statements, one by Paul and the other by Moses, appear to conflict. Paul declares, "Whosoever shall do the works of the Law, is accursed." Moses declares, "Whosoever shall not do the works of the Law, is accursed." How can these two contradictory statements be reconciled? How can the one statement prove the other? No person can hope to understand Paul unless he understands the article of justification. These two statements are not at all inconsistent.

We must bear in mind that to do the works of the Law does not mean only to live up to the superficial requirements of the Law, but to obey the spirit of the Law to perfection. But where will you find the person who can do that? Let him step forward and we will praise him.

Our opponents have their answer ready-made. They quote Paul's own statement in Romans 2:13, "The doers of the law shall be justified." Very well. But let us first find out who the doers of the law are. They call a "doer" of the Law one who performs the Law in its literal sense. This is not to "do" the Law. This is to sin. When our opponents go about to perform the Law, they sin against the first, the second, and the third commandments; in fact they sin against the whole Law. For God requires above all that we worship Him in spirit and in faith. In observing the Law for the purpose of obtaining righteousness without faith in Christ these law-workers go smack against the Law and against God. They deny the righteousness of God, His mercy, and His promises. They deny Christ and all His benefits.

In their ignorance of the true purpose of the Law the exponents of the Law abuse the Law, as Paul says, Romans 10:3, "For they, being ignorant of God's righteousness, and going about to establish their own righteousness, have not submitted themselves unto the righteousness of God."

In their folly our opponents rush into the Scriptures, pick out a sentence here and a sentence there about the Law and imagine they know all about it. Their work-righteousness is plain idolatry and blasphemy against God. No wonder they abide under the curse of God.

Because God saw that we could not fulfill the Law, He provided a way of salvation long before the Law was ever given, a salvation that He promised to Abraham, saying, "In thee shall all nations be blessed."

The very first thing for us to do is to believe in Christ. First, we must receive the Holy Spirit, who enlightens and sanctifies us so that we can begin to do the Law, i.e., to love God and our neighbor. Now, the Holy Ghost is not obtained by the Law, but by faith in Christ. In the last analysis, to do the

Law means to believe in Jesus Christ. The tree comes first, and then come the fruits.

The scholastics admit that a mere external and superficial performance of the Law without sincerity and good will is plain hypocrisy. Judas acted like the other disciples. What was wrong with Judas? Mark what Rome answers, "Judas was a reprobate. His motives were perverse, therefore his works were hypocritical and no good." Well, well. Rome does admit, after all, that works in themselves do not justify unless they issue from a sincere heart. Why do our opponents not profess the same truth in spiritual matters? There, above all, faith must precede everything. The heart must be purified by faith before a person can lift a finger to please God.

There are two classes of doers of the Law, true doers and hypocritical doers. The true doers of the Law are those who are moved by faith in Christ to do the Law. The hypocritical doers of the Law are those who seek to obtain righteousness by a mechanical performance of good works while their hearts are far removed from God. They act like the foolish carpenter who starts with the roof when he builds a house. Instead of doing the Law, these law-conscious hypocrites break the Law. They break the very first commandment of God by denying His promise in Christ. They do not worship God in faith. They worship themselves.

No wonder Paul was able to foretell the abominations that Antichrist would bring into the Church. That Antichrists would come, Christ Himself prophesied, Matthew 24:5, "For many shall come in my name, saying, I am Christ; and shall deceive many." Whoever seeks righteousness by works denies God and makes himself God. He is an Antichrist because he ascribes to his own works the omnipotent capability of conquering sin, death, devil, hell, and the wrath of God. An Antichrist lays claim to the honor of Christ. He is an idolater of himself. The law-righteous person is the worst kind of infidel.

Those who intend to obtain righteousness by their own efforts do not say in so many words: "I am God; I am Christ." But it amounts to that. They usurp the divinity and office of Christ. The effect is the same as if they said, "I am Christ; I am a Savior. I save myself and others." This is the impression the monks give out.

The Pope is the Antichrist, because he is against Christ, because he takes liberties with the things of God, because he lords it over the temple of God.

I cannot tell you in words how criminal it is to seek righteousness before God without faith in Christ, by the works of the Law. It is the abomination standing in the holy place. It deposes the Creator and deifies the creature.

The real doers of the Law are the true believers. The Holy Spirit enables them to love God and their neighbor. But because we have only the first-fruits of the Spirit and not the tenth-fruits, we do not observe the Law perfectly. This imperfection of ours, however, is not imputed to us, for Christ's sake.

Hence, the statement of Moses, "Cursed is every one that continueth not in all things which are written in the book of the law to do them," is not contrary to Paul. Moses requires perfect doers of the Law. But where will you find them? Nowhere. Moses himself confessed that he was not a perfect doer of the Law. He said to the Lord: "Pardon our iniquity and our sin." Christ alone can make us innocent of any transgression. How so? First, by the forgiveness of our sins and the imputation of His righteousness. Secondly, by the gift of the Holy Ghost, who engenders new life and activity in us.

Objections to the Doctrine of Faith Disproved

Here we shall take the time to enter upon the objections which our opponents raise against the doctrine of faith. There are many passages in the Bible that deal with works and the reward of works which our opponents cite against us in the belief that these will disprove the doctrine of faith which we teach.

The scholastics grant that according to the reasonable order of nature being precedes doing. They grant that any act is faulty unless it proceeds from a right motive. They grant that a person must be right before he can do right. Why don't they grant that the right inclination of the heart toward God through faith in Christ must precede works?

In the eleventh chapter of the Epistle to the Hebrews we find a catalogue of various works and deeds of the saints of the Bible. David, who killed a lion and a bear, and defeated Goliath, is mentioned. In the heroic deeds of David the scholastic can discover nothing more than outward achievement. But the deeds of David must be evaluated according to the personality of David. When we understand that David was a man of faith, whose heart trusted in the Lord, we shall understand why he could do such heroic deeds. David said: "The Lord that delivered me out of the paw of the lion, and out of the paw of the bear, he will deliver me out of the hand of this Philistine." Again: "Thou comest to me with a sword, and with a spear, and with a shield: but I come to thee in the name of the Lord of hosts, the God of the armies of Israel, whom thou hast defied. This day will the Lord deliver thee into mine hand; and I will smite thee, and take thine head from thee" (I Samuel 17:37, 45, 46). Before David could achieve a single heroic deed he was already a man beloved of God, strong and constant in faith.

Of Abel it is said in the same Epistle: "By faith Abel offered unto God a more excellent sacrifice than Cain." When the scholastics come upon the parallel passage in Genesis 4:4, they get no further than the words: "And the Lord had respect unto Abel and to his offering." "Aha!" they cry. "See, God has respect to offerings. Works do justify." With mud in their eyes they cannot see that the text says in Genesis that the Lord had respect to the person of Abel first. Abel pleased the Lord because of his faith. Because the person of Abel pleased the Lord, the offering of Abel pleased the Lord also. The Epistle to the Hebrews expressly states: "By faith Abel offered unto God a more excellent sacrifice."

In our dealings with God the work is worth nothing without faith, for "without faith it is impossible to please him" (Hebrews 11:6). The sacrifice of Abel was better than the sacrifice of Cain, because Abel had faith. As to Cain he had no faith or trust in God's grace, but strutted about in his own fancied worth. When God refused to recognize Cain's worth, Cain got angry at God and at Abel.

The Holy Spirit speaks of faith in different ways in the Sacred Scriptures. Sometimes He speaks of faith independently of other matters. When the Scriptures speak of faith in the absolute or abstract, faith refers to justification directly. But when the Scripture speaks of rewards and works it speaks of compound or relative faith. We will furnish some examples. Galatians 5:6, "Faith which worketh by love." Leviticus 18:5, "Which if a man do, he shall live in them." Matthew 19:17, "If thou wilt enter into life, keep the commandments." Psalm 37:27, "Depart from evil, and do good." In these and other passages where mention is made of doing, the Scriptures always speak of a faith-ful doing, a doing inspired by faith. "Do this and thou shalt live,," means: First have faith in Christ, and Christ will enable you to do and to live.

In the Word of God all things that are attributed to works are attributable to faith. Faith is the divinity of works. Faith permeates all the deeds of the believer, as Christ's divinity permeated His humanity. Abraham was accounted righteous because faith pervaded his whole personality and his every action.

When you read how the fathers, prophets, and kings accomplished great deeds, remember to explain them as the Epistle to the Hebrews accounts for them: "Who through faith subdued kingdoms, wrought righteousness, obtained promises, stopped the mouths of lions" (Hebrews 11:33). In this way will we correctly interpret all those passages that seem to support the righteousness of works. The Law is truly observed only through faith. Hence, every "holy," "moral" law-worker is accursed.

Supposing that this explanation will not satisfy the scholastics, supposing that they should completely wrap me up in their arguments (they cannot do it), I would rather be wrong and give all credit to Christ alone. Here is

Christ. Paul, Christ's apostle, declares that "Christ hath redeemed us from the curse of the law, being made a curse for us" (Gal. 3:13). I hear with my own ears that I cannot be saved except by the blood and death of Christ. I conclude, therefore, that it is up to Christ to overcome my sins, and not up to the Law, or my own efforts. If He is the price of my redemption, if He was made sin for my justification, I don't give a care if you quote me a thousand Scripture passages for the righteousness of works against the righteousness of faith. I have the Author and Lord of the Scriptures on my side. I would rather believe Him than all that riffraff of "pious" law-workers.

Verse 11. But that no man is justified by the law in the sight of God, it is evident: for, The just shall live by faith.

The Apostle draws into his argument the testimony of the Prophet Habak-kuk: "The just shall live by his faith." This passage carries much weight because it eliminates the Law and the deeds of the Law as factors in the process of our justification.

The scholastics misconstrue this passage by saying: "The just shall live by faith, if it is a working faith, or a faith formed and performed by charitable works." Their annotation is a forgery. To speak of formed or unformed faith, a sort of double faith, is contrary to the Scriptures. If charitable works can form and perfect faith I am forced to say eventually that charitable deeds constitute the essential factor in the Christian religion. Christ and His benefits would be lost to us.

Verse 12. And the law is not of faith.

In direct opposition to the scholastics Paul declares: "The law is not of faith." What is this charity the scholastics talk so much about? Does not the Law command charity? The fact is the Law commands nothing but charity, as we may gather from the following Scripture passages: "Thou shalt love the Lord thy God with all thine heart, and with all thy soul, and with all thy might" (Deut. 6:5). "Shewing mercy unto thousands of them that love me, and keep my commandments" (Exodus 20:6). "On these two commandments hang all the law and the prophets" (Matt. 22:40). If the law requires charity, charity is part of the Law and not of faith. Since Christ has displaced the Law which commands charity, it follows that charity has been abrogated with the Law as a factor in our justification, and only faith is left.

Verse 12. But, The man that doeth them shall live in them.

Paul undertakes to explain the difference between the righteousness of the Law and the righteousness of faith. The righteousness of the Law is the fulfillment of the Law according to the passage: "The man that doeth them shall live in them." The righteousness of faith is to believe the Gospel according to the passage: "The just shall live by faith." The Law is a statement of debit, the Gospel a statement of credit. By this distinction Paul explains why charity which is the commandment of the Law cannot justify, because the Law contributes nothing to our justification.

Indeed, works do follow after faith, but faith is not therefore a meritorious work. Faith is a gift. The character and limitations of the Law must be rigidly maintained.

When we believe in Christ we live by faith. When we believe in the Law we may be active enough but we have no life. The function of the Law is not to give life; the function of the Law is to kill. True, the Law says: "The man that doeth them shall live in them." But where is the person who can do "them," i.e., love God with all his heart, soul, and mind, and his neighbor as himself?

Paul has nothing against those who are justified by faith and therefore are true doers of the Law. He opposes those who think they can fulfill the Law when in reality they can only sin against the Law by trying to obtain righteousness by the Law. The Law demands that we fear, love, and worship God with a true faith. The law-workers fail to do this. Instead, they invent new modes of worship and new kinds of works which God never commanded. They provoke His anger according to the passage: "But in vain they do worship me, teaching for doctrines the commandments of men" (Matthew 15:9). Hence, the law-righteous workers are downright rebels against God, and idolaters who constantly sin against the first commandment. In short, they are no good at all though outwardly they seem to be extremely solicitous of the honor of God.

We who are justified by faith as the saints of old, may be under the Law, but we are not under the curse of the Law because sin is not imputed to us for Christ's sake. If the Law cannot be fulfilled by the believers, if sin continues to cling to them despite their love for God, what can you expect of people who are not yet justified by faith, who are still enemies of God and His Word, like the unbelieving law-workers? It goes to show how impossible it is for those who have not been justified by faith to fulfill the Law.

Verse 13. Christ hath redeemed us from the curse of the law, being made a curse for us: for it is written, Cursed is every one that hangeth on a tree.

Jerome and his present-day followers rack their miserable brains over this comforting passage in an effort to save Christ from the fancied insult of being called a curse. They say: "This quotation from Moses does not apply to Christ. Paul is taking liberties with Moses by generalizing the statements in Deuteronomy 21:23. Moses has 'he that is hanged.' Paul puts it 'every one that hangeth.' On the other hand, Paul omits the words 'of God' in his quotation from Moses: 'For he that is hanged is accursed of God.' Moses speaks of a criminal who is worthy of death." "How," our opponents ask, "can this passage be applied to the holy Christ as if He were accursed of God and worthy to be hanged?" This piece of exegesis may impress the naive as a zealous attempt to defend the honor and glory of Christ. Let us see what Paul has in mind.

Paul does not say that Christ was made a curse for Himself. The accent is on the two words "for us." Christ is personally innocent. Personally, He did not deserve to be hanged for any crime of His own doing. But because Christ took the place of others who were sinners, He was hanged like any other transgressor. The Law of Moses leaves no loopholes. It says that a transgressor should be hanged. Who are the other sinners? We are. The sentence of death and everlasting damnation had long been pronounced over us. But Christ took all our sins and died for them on the Cross. "He was numbered with the transgressors; and he bare the sin of many, and made intercession for the transgressors" (Isaiah 53:12).

All the prophets of old said that Christ should be the greatest transgressor, murderer, adulterer, thief, blasphemer that ever was or ever could be on earth. When He took the sins of the whole world upon Himself, Christ was no longer an innocent person. He was a sinner burdened with the sins of a Paul who was a blasphemer; burdened with the sins of a Peter who denied Christ; burdened with the sins of a David who committed adultery and murder, and gave the heathen occasion to laugh at the Lord. In short, Christ was charged with the sins of all men, that He should pay for them with His own blood. The curse struck Him. The Law found Him among sinners. He was not only in the company of sinners. He had gone so far as to invest Himself with the flesh and blood of sinners. So the Law judged and hanged Him for a sinner.

In separating Christ from us sinners and holding Him up as a holy exemplar, errorists rob us of our best comfort. They misrepresent Him as a threatening tyrant who is ready to slaughter us at the slightest provocation.

I am told that it is preposterous and wicked to call the Son of God a cursed sinner. I answer: If you deny that He is a condemned sinner, you are forced to deny that Christ died. It is not less preposterous to say, the Son of God died, than to say, the Son of God was a sinner.

John the Baptist called Him "the lamb of God, which taketh away the sin of the world." Being the unspotted Lamb of God, Christ was personally innocent. But because He took the sins of the world, His sinlessness was defiled with the sinfulness of the world. Whatever sins I, you, all of us have committed or shall commit, they are Christ's sins as if He had committed them Himself. Our sins have to be Christ's sins or we shall perish forever.

Isaiah declares of Christ: "The Lord hath laid on him the iniquity of us all." We have no right to minimize the force of this declaration. God does not amuse Himself with words. What a relief for a Christian to know that Christ is covered all over with my sins, your sins, and the sins of the whole world.

The papists invented their own doctrine of faith. They say charity creates and adorns their faith. By stripping Christ of our sins, by making Him sinless, they cast our sins back at us, and make Christ absolutely worthless to us. What sort of charity is this? If that is a sample of their vaunted charity, we want none of it.

Our merciful Father in heaven saw how the Law oppressed us and how impossible it was for us to get out from under the curse of the Law. He therefore sent His only Son into the world and said to Him: "You are now Peter, the liar; Paul, the persecutor; David, the adulterer; Adam, the disobedient; the thief on the cross. You, My Son, must pay the world's iniquity." The Law growls: "All right. If Your Son is taking the sin of the world, I see no sins anywhere else but in Him. He shall die on the Cross." And the Law kills Christ. But we go free.

The argument of the Apostle against the righteousness of the Law is impregnable. If Christ bears our sins, we do not bear them. But if Christ is innocent of our sins and does not bear them, we must bear them, and we shall die in our sins. "But thanks be to God, which giveth us the victory through our Lord Jesus Christ."

Let us see how Christ was able to gain the victory over our enemies. The sins of the whole world, past, present, and future, fastened themselves upon Christ and condemned Him. But because Christ is God, He had an everlasting and unconquerable righteousness. These two, the sin of the world and the righteousness of God, met in a death struggle. Furiously the sin of the world assailed the righteousness of God. Righteousness is immortal and invincible. On the other hand, sin is a mighty tyrant who subdues all men. This tyrant pounces on Christ. But Christ's righteousness is unconquerable. The result is inevitable. Sin is defeated and righteousness triumphs and reigns forever.

In the same manner was death defeated. Death is emperor of the world. He strikes down kings, princes, all men. He has an idea to destroy all life. But Christ has immortal life, and life immortal gained the victory over death. Through Christ death has lost her sting. Christ is the Death of death.

The curse of God waged a similar battle with the eternal mercy of God in Christ. The curse meant to condemn God's mercy. But it could not do it because the mercy of God is everlasting. The curse had to give way. If the mercy of God in Christ had lost out, God Himself would have lost out, which, of course, is impossible.

"Christ," says Paul, "spoiled principalities and powers, He made a show of them openly, triumphing over them in it" (Col. 2:15). They cannot harm those who hide in Christ. Sin, death, the wrath of God, hell, and the devil are mortified in Christ. Where Christ is near the powers of evil must keep their distance. St. John says: "And this is the victory that overcometh the world, even our faith" (I John 5:4).

You may now perceive why it is imperative to believe and confess the divinity of Christ. To overcome the sin of a whole world, and death, and the wrath of God was no work for any creature. The power of sin and death could be broken only by a greater power. God alone could abolish sin, destroy death, and take away the curse of the Law. God alone could bring righteousness, life, and mercy to light. In attributing these achievements to Christ the Scriptures pronounce Christ to be God forever. The article of justification is indeed fundamental. If we remain sound in this one article, we remain sound in all the other articles of the Christian faith. When we teach justification by faith in Christ we confess at the same time that Christ is God.

I cannot get over the blindness of the Pope's theologians. To imagine that the mighty forces of sin, death, and the curse can be vanquished by the righteousness of man's paltry works, by fasting, pilgrimages, masses, vows, and such gewgaws. These blind leaders of the blind turn the poor people over to the mercy of sin, death, and the devil. What chance has a defenseless human creature against these powers of darkness? They train sinners who are ten times worse than any thief, whore, murderer. The divine power of God alone can destroy sin and death, and create righteousness and life.

When we hear that Christ was made a curse for us, let us believe it with joy and assurance. By faith Christ changes places with us. He gets our sins, we get His holiness.

By faith alone can we become righteous, for faith invests us with the sinlessness of Christ. The more fully we believe this, the fuller will be our joy. If you believe that sin, death, and the curse are void, why, they are null, zero. Whenever sin and death make you nervous, write it down as an illusion of the devil. There is no sin now, no curse, no death, no devil because Christ has done away with them. This fact is sure. There is nothing wrong with the fact. The defect lies in our lack of faith.

In the Apostolic Creed we confess: "I believe in the holy Christian Church." That means, I believe that there is no sin, no curse, no evil in the Church of God. Faith says: "I believe that." But if you want to believe your eyes, you will find many shortcomings and offenses in the members of the holy Church. You see them succumb to temptation, you see them weak in faith, you see them giving way to anger, envy, and other evil dispositions. "How can the Church be holy?" you ask. It is with the Christian Church as it is with the individual Christian. If I examine myself, I find enough unholiness to shock me. But when I look at Christ in me, I find that I am altogether holy. And so it is with the Church.

Holy Writ does not say that Christ was under the curse. It says directly that Christ was made a curse. In II Corinthians 5:21 Paul writes: "For he (God) hath made him (Christ) to be sin for us, who knew no sin; that we might be made the righteousness of God in him." Although this and similar passages may be properly explained by saying that Christ was made a sacrifice for the curse and for sin, yet in my judgment it is better to leave these passages stand as they read: Christ was made sin itself; Christ was made the curse itself. When a sinner gets wise to himself, he does not only feel miserable, he feels like misery personified; he does not only feel like a sinner, he feels like sin itself.

To finish with this verse: All evils would have overwhelmed us, as they shall overwhelm the unbelievers forever, if Christ had not become the great transgressor and guilty bearer of all our sins. The sins of the world got Him down for a moment. They came around Him like water. Of Christ, the Old Testament Prophet complained: "Thy fierce wrath goeth over me; thy terrors have cut me off" (Psalm 88:16). By Christ's salvation we have been delivered from the terrors of God to a life of eternal felicity.

Verse 14. That the blessing of Abraham might come on the Gentiles through Jesus Christ.

Paul always keeps this text before him: "In thy seed shall all the nations of the earth be blessed." The blessing promised unto Abraham could come upon the Gentiles only by Christ, the seed of Abraham. To become a blessing unto all nations Christ had to be made a curse to take away the curse from the nations of the earth. The merit that we plead, and the work that we proffer is Christ who was made a curse for us.

Let us become expert in the art of transferring our sins, our death, and every evil from ourselves to Christ; and Christ's righteousness and blessing from Christ to ourselves.

Verse 14. That we might receive the promise of the Spirit through faith.

"The promise of the Spirit" is Hebrew for "the promised Spirit." The Spirit spells freedom from the Law, sin, death, the curse, hell, and the judgment of God. No merits are mentioned in connection with this promise of the

Spirit and all the blessings that go with Him. This Spirit of many blessings is received by faith alone. Faith alone builds on the promises of God, as Paul says in this verse.

Long ago the prophets visualized the happy changes Christ would effect in all things. Despite the fact that the Jews had the Law of God they never ceased to look longingly for Christ. After Moses no prophet or king added a single law to the Book. Any changes or additions were deferred to the time of Christ's coming. Moses told the people: "The Lord thy God will raise up unto thee a Prophet from the midst of thee, of thy brethren, like unto me; unto him ye shall hearken" (Deut. 18:15).

God's people of old felt that the Law of Moses could not be improved upon until the Messiah would bring better things than the Law, i.e., grace and remission of sins.

Verse 15. Brethren, I speak after the manner of men; Though it be but a man's covenant, yet if it be confirmed, no man disannulleth, or addeth thereto.

After the preceding, well-taken argument, Paul offers another based on the similarity between a man's testament and God's testament. A man's testament seems too weak a premise for the Apostle to argue from in confirmation of so important a matter as justification. We ought to prove earthly things by heavenly things, and not heavenly things by earthly things. But where the earthly thing is an ordinance of God, we may use it to prove divine matters. In Matthew 7:11 Christ Himself argued from earthly to heavenly things when He said: "If ye then, being evil, know how to give good gifts to your children, how much more shall your Father which is in heaven give good things to them that ask him?"

To come to Paul's argument. Civil law, which is God's ordinance, prohibits tampering with any testament of man. Any person's last will and testament must be respected. Paul asks: "Why is it that man's last will is scrupulously respected and not God's testament? You would not think of breaking faith with a man's testament. Why do you not keep faith with God's testament?"

The Apostle says that he is speaking after the manner of men. He means to say: "I will give you an illustration from the customs of men. If a man's last will is respected, and it is, how much more ought the testament of God be honored: 'In thy seed shall all the nations of the earth be blessed.' When Christ died, this testament was sealed by His blood. After His death the testament was opened, it was published to the nations. No man ought to alter God's testament as the false apostles do who substitute the Law and traditions of men for the testament of God."

As the false prophets tampered with God's testament in the days of Paul, so many do in our day. They will observe human laws punctiliously, but the laws of God they transgress without the flicker of an eyelid. But the time will come when they will find out that it is no joke to pervert the testament of God.

Verse 16. Now to Abraham and his seed were the promises made. He saith not, And to seeds, as of many; but as of one, And to thy seed, which is Christ.

The word testament is another name for the promise that God made unto Abraham concerning Christ. A testament is not a law, but an inheritance. Heirs do not look for laws and assessments when they open a last will; they look for grants and favors. The testament which God made out to Abraham did not contain laws. It contained promises of great spiritual blessings.

The promises were made in view of Christ, in one seed, not in many seeds. The Jews will not accept this interpretation. They insist that the singular "seed" is put for the plural "seeds." We prefer the interpretation of Paul, who makes a fine case for Christ and for us out of the singular "seed," and is after all inspired to do so by the Holy Ghost.

Verse 17. And this I say, that the covenant, that was confirmed before of God in Christ, the law which was four hundred and thirty years after, cannot disannul, that it should make the promise of none effect.

The Jews assert that God was not satisfied with His promises, but after four hundred and thirty years He gave the Law. "God," they say, "must have mistrusted His own promises, and considered them inadequate for salvation. Therefore He added to His promises something better, the Law. The Law," they say, "canceled the promises."

Paul answers: "The Law was given four hundred and thirty years after the promise was made to Abraham. The Law could not cancel the promise because the promise was the testament of God, confirmed by God in Christ many years before the Law. What God has once promised He does not take back. Every promise of God is a ratified promise."

Why was the Law added to the promise? Not to serve as a medium by which the promise might be obtained. The Law was added for these reasons: That there might be in the world a special people, rigidly controlled by the Law, a people out of which Christ should be born in due time; and that men burdened by many laws might sigh and long for Him, their Redeemer, the seed of Abraham. Even the ceremonies prescribed by the Law foreshadowed Christ. Therefore the Law was never meant to cancel the promise of God. The Law was meant to confirm the promise until the time should come when God would open His testament in the Gospel of Jesus Christ.

God did well in giving the promise so many years before the Law, that it may never be said that righteousness is granted through the Law and not through the promise. If God had meant for us to be justified by the Law, He would have given the Law four hundred and thirty years before the promise, at least He would have given the Law at the same time He gave the promise. But He never breathed a word about the Law until four hundred years after. The promise is therefore better than the Law. The Law does not cancel the promise, but faith in the promised Christ cancels the Law.

The Apostle is careful to mention the exact number of four hundred and thirty years. The wide divergence in the time between the promise and the Law helps to clinch Paul's argument that righteousness is not obtained by the Law.

Let me illustrate. A man of great wealth adopts a strange lad for his son. Remember, he does not owe the lad anything. In due time he appoints the lad heir to his entire fortune. Several years later the old man asks the lad to do something for him. And the young lad does it. Can the lad then go around and say that he deserved the inheritance by his obedience to the old man's request? How can anybody say that righteousness is obtained by obedience to the Law when the Law was given four hundred and thirty years after God's promise of the blessing?

One thing is certain, Abraham was never justified by the Law, for the simple reason that the Law was not in his day. If the Law was non-existent how could Abraham obtain righteousness by the Law? Abraham had nothing else to go by but the promise. This promise he believed and that was counted unto him for righteousness. If the father obtained righteousness through faith, the children get it the same way.

We use the argument of time also. We say our sins were taken away by the death of Christ fifteen hundred years ago, long before there were any religious orders, canons, or rules of penance, merits, etc. What did people do about their sins before these new inventions were hatched up?

Paul finds his arguments for the righteousness of faith everywhere. Even the element of time serves to build his case against the false apostles. Let us fortify our conscience with similar arguments. They help us in the trials of our faith. They turn our attention from the Law to the promises, from sin to righteousness; from death to life.

It is not for nothing that Paul bears down on this argument. He foresaw this confusion of the promise and the Law creeping into the Church. Accustom yourself to separate Law and Gospel even in regard to time. When 123the Law comes to pay your conscience a visit, say: "Mister Law, you come too soon. The four hundred and thirty years aren't up yet. When they are up, you come again. Won't you?"

Verse 18. For if the inheritance be of the law, it is no more of promise.

In Romans 4:14, the Apostle writes: "For if they which are made of the law be heirs, faith is made void, and the promise made of none effect." It cannot be otherwise. That the Law is something entirely different from the promise is plain. The Law thunders: "Thou shalt, thou shalt not." The promise of the "seed" pleads: "Take this gift of God." If the inheritance of the gifts of God were obtained by the Law, God would be a liar. We would have the right to ask Him: "Why did you make this promise in the first place: 'In thy seed shall all the nations of the earth be blessed'? Why did you not say: 'In thy works thou shalt be blessed'?"

Verse 18. But God gave it to Abraham by promise.

So much is certain, before the Law ever existed, God gave Abraham the inheritance or blessing by the promise. In other words, God granted unto Abraham remission of sins, righteousness, salvation, and everlasting life. And not only to Abraham but to all believers, because God said: "In thy seed shall all the nations of the earth be blessed." The blessing was given unconditionally. The Law had no chance to butt in because Moses was not yet born. "How then can you say that righteousness is obtained by the Law?"

The Apostle now goes to work to explain the province and purpose of the Law.

Verse 19. Wherefore then serveth the law?

The question naturally arises: If the Law was not given for righteousness or salvation, why was it given? Why did God give the Law in the first place if it cannot justify a person?

The Jews believed if they kept the Law they would be saved. When they heard that the Gospel proclaimed a Christ who had come into the world to save sinners and not the righteous; when they heard that sinners were to enter the kingdom of heaven before the righteous, the Jews were very much put out. They murmured: "These last have wrought but one hour, and thou hast made them equal unto us, which have borne the burden and heat of the day" (Matthew 20:12). They complained that the heathen who at one time had been worshipers of idols obtained grace without the drudgery of the Law that was theirs.

Today we hear the same complaints. "What was the use of our having lived in a cloister, twenty, thirty, forty years; what was the sense of having vowed chastity, poverty, obedience; what good are all the masses and canonical hours that we read; what profit is there in fasting, praying, etc., if any man or woman, any beggar or scour woman is to be made equal to us, or even be considered more acceptable unto God than we?"

Reason takes offense at the statement of Paul: "The law was added because of transgressions." People say that Paul abrogated the Law, that he is a radical, that he blasphemed God when he said that. People say: "We might as well live like wild people if the Law does not count. Let us abound in sin that grace may abound. Let us do evil that good may come of it."

What are we to do? Such scoffing distresses us, but we cannot stop it. Christ Himself was accused of being a blasphemer and rebel. Paul and all the other apostles were told the same things. Let the scoffers slander us, let them spare us not. But we must not on their own account keep silent. We must speak frankly in order that afflicted consciences may find surcease. Neither are we to pay any attention to the foolish and ungodly people for abusing our doctrine. They are the kind that would scoff, Law or no Law. Our first consideration must be the comfort of troubled consciences, that they may not perish with the multitudes.

When he saw that some were offended at his doctrine, while others found in it encouragement to live after the flesh, Paul comforted himself with the thought that it was his duty to preach the Gospel to the elect of God, and that for their sake he must endure all things. Like Paul we also do all these things for the sake of God's elect. As for the scoffers and skeptics, I am so disgusted with them that in all my life I would not open my mouth for them once. I wish that they were back there where they belong under the iron heel of the Pope.

People foolish but wise in their conceits jump to the conclusion: If the Law does not justify, it is good for nothing. How about that? Because money does not justify, would you say that money is good for nothing? Because the eyes do not justify, would you have them taken out? Because the Law does not justify it does not follow that the Law is without value. We must find and define the proper purpose of the Law. We do not offhand condemn the Law because we say it does not justify.

We say with Paul that the Law is good if it is used properly. Within its proper sphere the Law is an excellent thing. But if we ascribe to the Law functions for which it was never intended, we pervert not only the Law but also the Gospel.

It is the universal impression that righteousness is obtained through the deeds of the Law. This impression is instinctive and therefore doubly dangerous. Gross sins and vices may be recognized or else repressed by the threat of punishment. But this sin, this opinion of man's own righteousness refuses to be classified as sin. It wants to be esteemed as high-class religion. Hence, it constitutes the mighty influence of the devil over the entire world. In order to point out the true office of the Law, and thus to stamp out that false impression of the righteousness of 126the Law, Paul answers the question: "Wherefore then serveth the Law?" with the words:

Verse 19. It was added because of transgressions.

All things differ. Let everything serve its unique purpose. Let the sun shine by day, the moon and the stars by night. Let the sea furnish fish, the earth grain, the woods trees, etc. Let the Law also serve its unique purpose. It must not step out of character and take the place of anything else. What is the function of the Law? "Transgression," answers the Apostle.

The Twofold Purpose of the Law

The Law has a twofold purpose. One purpose is civil. God has ordained civil laws to punish crime. Every law is given to restrain sin. Does it not then make men righteous? No. In refraining from murder, adultery, theft, or other sins, I do so under compulsion because I fear the jail, the noose, the electric chair. These restrain me as iron bars restrain a lion and a bear. Otherwise they would tear everything to pieces. Such forceful restraint cannot be regarded as righteousness, rather as an indication of unrighteousness. As a wild beast is tied to keep it from running amuck, so the Law bridles mad and furious man to keep him from running wild. The need for restraint shows plainly enough that those who need the Law are not righteous, but wicked men who are fit to be tied. No, the Law does not justify.

The first purpose of the Law, accordingly, is to restrain the wicked. The devil gets people into all kinds of scrapes. Therefore God instituted governments, parents, laws, restrictions, and civil ordinances. At least they help to tie the devil's hands so that he does not rage up and down the earth. This civil restraint by the Law is intended by God for the preservation of all things, particularly for the good of the Gospel that it should not be hindered too much by the tumult of the wicked. But Paul is not now treating of this civil use and function of the Law.

The second purpose of the Law is spiritual and divine. Paul describes this spiritual purpose of the Law in the words, "Because of transgressions," i.e., to reveal to a person his sin, blindness, misery, his ignorance, hatred, and contempt of God, his death, hell, and condemnation.

This is the principal purpose of the Law and its most valuable contribution. As long as a person is not a murderer, adulterer, thief, he would swear that he is righteous. How is God going to humble such a person except by the Law? The Law is the hammer of death, the thunder of hell, and the lightning of God's wrath to bring down the proud and shameless hypocrites. When the Law was instituted on Mount Sinai it was accompanied by lightning, by storms, by the sound of trumpets, to tear to pieces that monster called self-righteousness. As long as a person thinks he is right he is going to be incomprehensibly proud and presumptuous. He is going to hate God, despise His grace and mercy, and ignore the promises in Christ. The Gospel of the free forgiveness of sins through Christ will never appeal to the self-righteous.

This monster of self-righteousness, this stiff-necked beast, needs a big axe. And that is what the Law is, a big axe. Accordingly, the proper use and function of the Law is to threaten until the conscience is scared stiff.

The awful spectacle at Mount Sinai portrayed the proper use of the Law. When the children of Israel came out of Egypt a feeling of singular holiness possessed them. They boasted: "We are the people of God. All that the Lord hath spoken we will do" (Ex. 19:8). This feeling of holiness was heightened when Moses ordered them to wash their clothes, to refrain from their wives, and to prepare themselves all around. The third day came and Moses led the people out of their tents to the foot of the mountain into the presence of the Lord. What happened? When the children of Israel saw the whole mountain burning and smoking, the black clouds rent by fierce lightning flashing up and down in the inky darkness, when they heard the sound of the trumpet blowing louder and longer, shattered by the roll of thunder, they were so frightened that they begged Moses: "Speak thou with us, and we will hear: but let not God speak with us, lest we die" (Ex. 20:19). I ask you, what good did their scrubbing, their snow-white clothes, and their continence do them? No good at all. Not a single one could stand in the presence of the glorious Lord. Stricken by the terror of God, they fled back into their tents, as if the devil were after them.

The Law is meant to produce the same effect today which it produced at Mount Sinai long ago. I want to encourage all who fear God, especially those who intend to become ministers of the Gospel, to learn from the Apostle the proper use of the Law. I fear that after our time the right handling of the Law will become a lost art. Even now, although we continually explain the separate functions of the Law and the Gospel, we have those among us who do not understand how the Law should be used. What will it be like when we are dead and gone?

We want it understood that we do not reject the Law as our opponents claim. On the contrary, we uphold the Law. We say the Law is good if it is used for the purposes for which it was designed, to check civil transgression, and to magnify spiritual transgressions. The Law is also a light like the Gospel. But instead of revealing the grace of God, righteousness, and life, the Law brings sin, death, and the wrath of God to light. This is the business of the Law, and here the business of the Law ends, and should go no further.

The business of the Gospel, on the other hand, is to quicken, to comfort, to raise the fallen. The Gospel carries the news that God for Christ's sake is merciful to the most unworthy sinners, if they will only believe that Christ by His death has delivered them from sin and everlasting death unto grace, forgiveness, and everlasting life. By keeping in mind the difference between the Law and the Gospel we let each perform its special task. Of this difference between the Law and the Gospel nothing can be discovered in the writings of the monks or scholastics, nor for that matter in the writings of the ancient fathers. Augustine understood the difference somewhat. Jerome and others knew nothing of it. The silence in the Church concerning the difference between the Law and the Gospel has resulted in untold harm. Unless a sharp distinction is maintained between the purpose and function of the Law and the Gospel, the Christian doctrine cannot be kept free from error.

Verse 19. It was added because of transgressions.

In other words, that transgressions might be recognized as such and thus increased. When sin, death, and the wrath of God are revealed to a person by the Law, he grows impatient, complains against God, and rebels. Before that he was a very holy man; he worshipped and praised God; he bowed his knees before God and gave thanks, like the Pharisee. But now that sin and death are revealed to him by the Law he wishes there were no God. The Law inspires hatred of God. Thus sin is not only revealed by the Law; sin is actually increased and magnified by the Law.

The Law is a mirror to show a person what he is like, a sinner who is guilty of death, and worthy of everlasting punishment. What is this bruising and beating by the hand of the Law to accomplish? This, that we may find the way to grace. The Law is an usher to lead the way to grace. God is the God of the humble, the miserable, the afflicted. It is His nature to exalt the humble, to comfort the sorrowing, to heal the broken-hearted, to justify the sinners, and to save the condemned. The fatuous idea that a person can be holy by himself denies God the pleasure of saving sinners. God must therefore first take the sledge-hammer of the Law in His fists and smash the beast of self-righteousness and its brood of self-confidence, self-wisdom, self-righteousness, and self-help. When the conscience has been thoroughly frightened by the Law it welcomes the Gospel of grace with its message of a Savior who came into the world, not to break the bruised reed, nor to quench the smoking flax, but to preach glad tidings to the poor, to heal the broken-hearted, and to grant forgiveness of sins to all the captives.

Man's folly, however, is so prodigious that instead of embracing the message of grace with its guarantee of the forgiveness of sin for Christ's sake, man finds himself more laws to satisfy his conscience. "If I live," says he, "I will mend my life. I will do this, I will do that." Man, if you don't do the very opposite, if you don't send Moses with the Law back to Mount Sinai and take the hand of Christ, pierced for your sins, you will never be saved.

When the Law drives you to the point of despair, let it drive you a little farther, let it drive you straight into the arms of Jesus who says: "Come unto me, all ye that labour and are heavy laden, and I will give you rest."

Verse 19. Till the seed should come to whom the promise was made.

The Law is not to have its say indefinitely. We must know how long the Law is to put in its licks. If it hammers away too long, no person would and could be saved. The Law has a boundary beyond which it must not go. How long ought the Law to hold sway? "Till the seed should come to whom the promise was made."

That may be taken literally to mean until the time of the Gospel. "From the days of John the Baptist," says Jesus, "until now the kingdom of heaven suffereth violence, and the violent take it by force. For all the prophets and the law prophesied until John" (Matthew 11:12, 13). When Christ came the Law and the ceremonies of Moses ceased.

Spiritually, it means that the Law is not to operate on a person after he has been humbled and frightened by the exposure of his sins and the wrath of God. We must then say to the Law: "Mister Law, lay off him. He has had enough. You scared him good and proper." Now it is the Gospel's turn. Now let Christ with His gracious lips talk to him of better things, grace, peace, forgiveness of sins, and eternal life.

Verse 19. And it was ordained by angels in the hand of a mediator.

The Apostle digresses a little from his immediate theme. Something occurred to him and he throws it in by the way. It occurred to him that the Law differs from the Gospel in another respect, in respect to authorship. The Law was delivered by the angels, but the Gospel by the Lord Himself. Hence, the Gospel is superior to the Law, as the word of a lord is superior to the word of his servant.

The Law was handed down by a being even inferior to the angels, by a middleman named Moses. Paul wants us to understand that Christ is the mediator of a better testament than mediator Moses of the Law. Moses led the people out of their tents to meet God. But they ran away. That is how good a mediator Moses was.

Paul says: "How can the Law justify when that whole sanctified people of Israel and even mediator Moses trembled at the voice of God? What kind of righteousness do you call that when people run away from it and hate it the worst way? If the Law could justify, people would love the Law. But look at the children of Israel running away from it."

The flight of the children of Israel from Mount Sinai indicates how people feel about the Law. They don't like it. If this were the only argument to prove that salvation is not by the Law, this one Bible history would do the work. What kind of righteousness is this law-righteousness when at the commencement exercises of the Law Moses and the scrubbed people run away from it so fast that an iron mountain, the Red Sea even, could not have stopped them until they were back in Egypt once again? If they could not hear the Law, how could they ever hope to perform the Law?

If all the world had stood at the mountain, all the world would have hated the Law and fled from it as the children of Israel did. The whole world is an enemy of the Law. How, then, can anyone be justified by the Law when everybody hates the Law and its divine author?

All this goes to show how little the scholastics know about the Law. They do not consider its spiritual effect and purpose, which is not to justify or to pacify afflicted consciences, but to increase sin, to terrify the conscience, and to produce wrath. In their ignorance the papists spout about man's good will and right judgment, and man's capacity to perform the Law of God. Ask the people of Israel who were present at the presentation of the Law on Mount Sinai whether what the scholastics say is true. Ask David, who often complains in the Psalms that he was cast away from God and in hell, that he was frantic about his sin, and sick at the thought of the wrath and judgment of God. No, the Law does not justify

Verse 20. Now a mediator is not a mediator of one.

Here the Apostle briefly compares the two mediators: Moses and Christ. "A mediator," says Paul, "is not a mediator of one." He is necessarily a mediator of two: The offender and the offended. Moses was such a mediator between the Law and the people who were offended at the Law. They were offended at the Law because they did not understand its purpose. That was the veil which Moses put over his face. The people were also offended at the Law because they could not look at the bare face of Moses. It shone with the glory of God. When Moses addressed the people he had to cover his face with that veil of his. They could not listen to their mediator Moses without another mediator, the veil. The Law had to change its face and voice. In other words, the Law had to be made tolerable to the people.

Thus covered, the Law no longer spoke to the people in its undisguised majesty. It became more tolerable to the conscience. This explains why men fail to understand the Law properly, with the result that they become secure and presumptuous hypocrites. One of two things has to be done: Either the Law must be covered with a veil and then it loses its full effectiveness, or it must be unveiled and then the full blast of its force kills. Man cannot stand the Law without a veil over it. Hence, we are forced either to look beyond the Law to Christ, or we go through life as shameless hypocrites and secure sinners.

Paul says: "A mediator is not a mediator of one." Moses could not be a mediator of God only, for God needs no mediator. Again, Moses could not be a mediator of the people only. He was a mediator between God and the people. It is the office of a mediator to conciliate the party that is offended and to placate the party that is the offender. However, Moses' mediation consisted only in changing the tone of the Law to make it more tolerable to the people. Moses was merely a mediator of the veil. He could not supply the ability to perform the Law.

What do you suppose would have happened if the Law had been given without a mediator and the people had been denied the services of a go-between? The people would have perished, or in case they had escaped they would have required the services of another mediator to preserve them alive and to keep the Law in force. Moses came along and he was made the mediator. He covered his face with a veil. But that is as much as he could do. He could not deliver men's consciences from the terror of the Law. The sinner needs a better mediator.

That better mediator is Jesus Christ. He does not change the voice of the Law, nor does He hide the Law with a veil. He takes the full blast of the wrath of the Law and fulfills its demands most meticulously.

Of this better Mediator Paul says: "A mediator is not a mediator of one." We are the offending party; God is the party offended. The offense is of such a nature that God cannot pardon it. Neither can we render adequate 134satisfaction for our offenses. There is discord between God and us. Could not God revoke His Law? No. How about running away from God? It cannot be done. It took Christ to come between us and God and to reconcile God to us. How did Christ do it? "Blotting out the handwriting of ordinances that was against us, which was contrary to us, and took it out of the way, nailing it to his cross" (Col. 2:14).

This one word, "mediator," is proof enough that the Law cannot justify. Otherwise we should not need a mediator.

In Christian theology the Law does not justify. In fact it has the contrary effect. The Law alarms us, it magnifies our sins until we begin to hate the Law and its divine Author. Would you call this being justified by the Law?

Can you imagine a more arrant outrage than to hate God and to abhor His Law? What an excellent Law it is. Listen: "I am the Lord thy God, which have brought thee out of the land of Egypt, out of the house of bondage. Thou shalt have no other gods . . . showing mercy unto thousands . . . honor thy father and thy mother: that thy days may be long upon the land . . ." (Ex. 20:2, 3, 6, 12). Are these not excellent laws, perfect wisdom? "Let not God speak with us, lest we die," cried the children of Israel. Is it not amazing that a person should refuse to hear things that are good for him? Any person would be glad to hear, I should think, that he has a gracious God who shows mercy unto thousands. Is it not amazing that people hate the Law that promotes their safety and welfare, e.g., "Thou shalt not kill; thou shalt not commit adultery; thou shalt not steal"?

The Law can do nothing for us except to arouse the conscience. Before the Law comes to me I feel no sin. But when the Law comes, sin, death, and hell are revealed to me. You would not call this being made righteous. You would call it being condemned to death and hell-fire.

Verse 20. But God is one.

God does not offend anybody, therefore He needs no mediator. But we offend God, therefore we need a mediator. And we need a better mediator than Moses. We need Christ.

Verse 21. Is the law then against the promises of God?

Before he digressed Paul stated that the Law does not justify. Shall we then discard the Law? No, no. It supplies a certain need. It supplies men with a needed realization of their sinfulness. Now arises another question: If the Law does no more than to reveal sin, does it not oppose the promises of God? The Jews believed that by the restraint and discipline of the Law the promises of God would be hastened, in fact earned by them.

Paul answers: "Not so. On the contrary, if we pay too much attention to the Law the promises of God will be slowed up. How can God fulfill His promises to a people that hates the Law?"

Verse 21. God forbid.

God never said to Abraham: "In thee shall all the nations of the earth be blessed because thou hast kept the Law." When Abraham was still uncircumcised and without the Law or any law, indeed, when he was still an idol worshiper, God said to him: "Get thee out of thy country, etc.; I am thy shield, etc.; In thy seed shall all the nations of the earth be blessed." These are unconditional promises which God freely made to Abraham without respect to works.

This is aimed especially at the Jews who think that the promises of God are impeded by their sins. Paul says: "The Lord is not slack concerning His promises because of our sins, or hastens His promises because of any merit on our part." God's promises are not influenced by our attitudes. They rest in His goodness and mercy.

Just because the Law increases sin, it does not therefore obstruct the promises of God. The Law confirms the promises, in that it prepares a person to look for the fulfillment of the promises of God in Christ.

The proverb has it that Hunger is the best cook. The Law makes afflicted consciences hungry for Christ. Christ tastes good to them. Hungry hearts appreciate Christ. Thirsty souls are what Christ wants. He invites them: "Come unto me, all ye that labour and are heavy laden, and I will give you rest." Christ's benefits are so precious that He will dispense them only to those who need them and really desire them.

Verse 21. For if there had been a law given which could have given life, verily righteousness should have been by the law.

The Law cannot give life. It kills. The Law does not justify a person before God; it increases sin. The Law does not secure righteousness; it hinders righteousness. The Apostle declares emphatically that the Law of itself cannot save.

Despite the intelligibility of Paul's statement, our enemies fail to grasp it. Otherwise they would not emphasize free will, natural strength, the works of supererogation, etc. To escape the charge of forgery they always have their convenient annotation handy, that Paul is referring only to the ceremonial and not to the moral law. But Paul includes all laws. He expressly says: "If there had been a law given."

There is no law by which righteousness may be obtained, not a single one. Why not?

Verse 22. But the Scripture hath concluded all under sin.

Where? First in the promises concerning Christ in Genesis 3:15 and in Genesis 22:18, which speak of the seed of the woman and the seed of Abraham. The fact that these promises were made unto the fathers concerning Christ implies that the fathers were subject to the curse of sin and eternal death. Otherwise why the need of promises?

Next, Holy Writ "concludes" all under sin in this passage from Paul: "For as many as are of the works of the law are under the curse." Again, in the passage which the Apostle quotes from Deuteronomy 27:26, "Cursed is every one that continueth not in all things which are written in the book of the law to do them." This passage clearly submits all men to the curse, not only those who sin openly against the Law, but also those who sincerely endeavor to perform the Law, inclusive of monks, friars, hermits, etc.

The conclusion is inevitable: Faith alone justified without works. If the Law itself cannot justify, much less can imperfect performance of the Law or the works of the Law, justify.

Verse 22. That the promise by faith of Jesus Christ might be given to them that believe.

The Apostle stated before that "the Scripture hath concluded all under sin." Forever? No, only until the promise should be fulfilled. The promise, you will recall, is the inheritance itself or the blessing promised to Abraham, deliverance from the Law, sin, death, and the devil, and the free gift of grace, righteousness, salvation, and eternal life. This promise, says Paul, is not obtained by any merit, by any law, or by any work. This promise is given. To whom? To those who believe. In whom? In Jesus Christ.

Verse 23. But before faith came.

The Apostle proceeds to explain the service which the Law is to render. Previously Paul had said that the Law was given to reveal the wrath and death of God upon all sinners. Although the Law kills, God brings good out of evil. He uses the Law to bring life. God saw that the universal illusion of self-righteousness could not be put down in any other way but by the Law. The Law dispels all self-illusions. It puts the fear of God in a man. Without this fear there can be no thirst for God's mercy. God accordingly uses the Law for a hammer to break up the illusion of self-righteousness, that we should despair of our own strength and efforts at self-justification.

Verse 23. But before faith came, we were kept under the law, shut up unto the faith which should afterwards be revealed.

The Law is a prison to those who have not as yet obtained grace. No prisoner enjoys the confinement. He hates it. If he could he would smash the prison and find his freedom at all cost. As long as he stays in prison he refrains from evil deeds. Not because he wants to, but because he has to. The bars and the chains restrain him. He does not regret the crime that put him in jail. On the contrary, he is mighty sore that he cannot rob and kill as before. If he could escape he would go right back to robbing and killing.

The Law enforces good behavior, at least outwardly. We obey the Law because if we don't we will be punished. Our obedience is inspired by fear. We obey under duress and we do it resentfully. Now what kind of righteousness is this when we refrain from evil out of fear of punishment? Hence, the righteousness of the Law is at bottom nothing but love of sin and hatred of righteousness.

All the same, the Law accomplishes this much, that it will outwardly at least and to a certain extent repress vice and crime.

But the Law is also a spiritual prison, a veritable hell. When the Law begins to threaten a person with death and the eternal wrath of God, a man just cannot find any comfort at all. He cannot shake off at will the nightmare of terror which the Law stirs up in his conscience. Of this terror of the Law the Psalms furnish many glimpses.

The Law is a civil and a spiritual prison. And such it should be. For that the Law is intended. Only the confinement in the prison of the Law must not be unduly prolonged. It must come to an end. The freedom of faith must succeed the imprisonment of the Law.

Happy the person who knows how to utilize the Law so that it serves the purposes of grace and of faith. Unbelievers are ignorant of this happy knowledge. When Cain was first shut up in the prison of the Law he felt no pang at the fratricide he had committed. He thought he could pass it off as an incident with a shrug of the shoulder. "Am I my brother's keeper?" he answered God flippantly. But when he heard the ominous words, "What hast thou done? the voice of thy brother's blood crieth unto me from the ground," Cain began to feel his imprisonment. Did he know how to get out of prison? No. He failed to call the Gospel to his aid. He said: "My punishment is greater than I can bear." He could only think of the prison. He forgot that he was brought face to face with his crime so that he should hurry to God for mercy and for pardon. Cain remained in the prison of the Law and despaired.

As a stone prison proves a physical handicap, so the spiritual prison of the Law proves a chamber of torture. But this it should only be until faith be revealed. The silly conscience must be educated to this. Talk to your conscience. Say: "Sister, you are now in jail all right. But you don't have to stay there forever. It is written that we are 'shut up unto faith which should afterwards be revealed.' Christ will lead you to freedom. Do not despair like Cain, Saul, or Judas. They might have gone free if they had called Christ to their aid. Just take it easy, Sister Conscience. It's good for you to be locked up for a while. It will teach you to appreciate Christ."

How anybody can say that he by nature loves the Law is beyond me. The Law is a prison to be feared and hated. Any unconverted person who says he loves the Law is a liar. He does not know what he is talking about. We love the Law about as well as a murderer loves his gloomy cell, his straight-jacket, and the iron bars in front of him. How then can the Law justify us?

Verse 23. Shut up unto the faith which should afterwards be revealed.

We know that Paul has reference to the time of Christ's coming. It was then that faith and the object of faith were fully revealed. But we may apply the historical fact to our inner life. When Christ came He abolished the Law and brought liberty and life to light. This He continues to do in the hearts of the believers. The Christian has a body in whose members, as Paul says, sin dwells and wars. I take sin to mean not only the deed but root, tree, fruit, and all. A Christian may perhaps not fall into the gross sins of murder, adultery, theft, but he is not free from impatience, complaints, hatreds, and blasphemy of God. As carnal lust is strong in a young man, in a man of full age the desire for glory, and in an old man covetousness, so impatience, doubt, and hatred of God often prevail in the hearts of sincere Christians. Examples of these sins may be garnered from the Psalms, Job, Jeremiah, and all the Sacred Scriptures.

Accordingly each Christian continues to experience in his heart times of the Law and times of the Gospel. The times of the Law are discernible by heaviness of heart, by a lively sense of sin, and a feeling of despair brought on by the Law. These periods of the Law will come again and again as long as we live. To mention my own case. There are many times when I find fault with God and am impatient with Him. The wrath and the judgment of God displease me, my wrath and impatience displease Him. Then is the season of the Law, when "the flesh lusteth against the Spirit, and the Spirit against the flesh." The time of grace returns when the heart is enlivened by the promise of God's mercy. It soliloquizes: "Why art thou cast down, O my soul? and why art thou disquieted within me? Can you see nothing but law, sin, death, and hell? Is there no grace, no forgiveness, no joy, peace, life, heaven, no Christ and God? Trouble me no more, my soul. Hope in God who has not spared His own dear Son but has given Him into death for thy sins." When the Law carries things too far, say: "Mister Law, you are not the whole show. There are other and better things than you. They tell me to trust in the Lord."

There is a time for the Law and a time for grace. Let us study to be good timekeepers. It is not easy. Law and grace may be miles apart in essence, but in the heart, they are pretty close together. In the heart fear and trust, sin and grace, Law and Gospel cross paths continually.

When reason hears that justification before God is obtained by grace alone,

it draws the inference that the Law is without value. The doctrine of the
Law must therefore be studied carefully lest we either reject the Law altogether, or are tempted to attribute to the Law a capacity to save. There are
three ways in which the Law may be abused. First, by the self-righteous
hypocrites who fancy that they can be justified by the Law. Secondly, by
those who claim that Christian liberty exempts a Christian from the ob-
servance of the Law. "These," says Peter, "use their liberty for a cloak of
maliciousness," and bring the name and the Gospel of Christ into ill repute.
Thirdly, the Law is abused by those who do not understand that the Law is
meant to drive us to Christ. When the Law is properly used its value cannot
be too highly appraised. It will take me to Christ every time.

Verse 24. Wherefore the law was our schoolmaster to bring us unto Christ.

This simile of the schoolmaster is striking. Schoolmasters are indispensable. But show me a pupil who loves his schoolmaster. How little love is lost
upon them the Jews showed by their attitude toward Moses. They would
have been glad to stone Moses to death (Ex. 17:4). You cannot expect
anything else. How can a pupil love a teacher who frustrates his desires?
And if the pupil disobeys, the schoolmaster whips him, and the pupil has
to like it and even kiss the rod with which he was beaten. Do you think the
schoolboy feels good about it? As soon as the teacher turns his back, the
pupil breaks the rod and throws it into the fire. And if he were stronger
than the teacher he would not take the beatings, but beat up the teacher. All
the same, teachers are indispensable, otherwise the children would grow up
without discipline, instruction, and training.

But how long are the scolding and the whippings of the schoolmaster to
continue? Only for a time, until the boy has been trained to be a worthy
heir of his father. No father wants his son to be whipped all the time. The
discipline is to last until the boy has been trained to be his father's worthy
successor.

The Law is such a schoolmaster. Not for always, but until we have been
brought to Christ. The Law is not just another schoolmaster. The Law is

a specialist to bring us to Christ. What would you think of a schoolmaster who could only torment and beat a child? Yet of such schoolmasters there were plenty in former times, regular bruisers. The Law is not that kind of a schoolmaster. It is not to torment us always. With its lashings it is only too anxious to drive us to Christ. The Law is like the good schoolmaster who trains his children to find pleasure in doing things they formerly detested.

Verse 24. That we might be justified by faith.

The Law is not to teach us another Law. When a person feels the full force of the Law he is likely to think: I have transgressed all the commandments of God; I am guilty of eternal death. If God will spare me I will change and live right from now on. This natural but entirely wrong reaction to the Law has bred the many ceremonies and works devised to earn grace and remission of sins.

The Law means to enlarge my sins, to make me small, so that I may be justified by faith in Christ. Faith is neither law nor word; but confidence in Christ "who is the end of the law." How so is Christ the end of the Law? Not in this way that He replaced the old Law with new laws. Nor is Christ the end of the Law in a way that 143makes Him a hard judge who has to be bribed by works as the papists teach. Christ is the end or finish of the Law to all who believe in Him. The Law can no longer accuse or condemn them.

AUGUSTINE: SELECTIONS FROM CITY OF GOD WRITTEN 413AD

Chapter 10.—That the Saints Lose Nothing in Losing Temporal Goods.

These are the considerations which one must keep in view, that he may answer the question whether any evil happens to the faithful and godly which cannot be turned to profit. Or shall we say that the question is needless, and that the apostle is vaporing when he says, "We know that all things work together for good to them that love God?"

They lost all they had. Their faith? Their godliness? The possessions of the hidden man of the heart, which in the sight of God are of great price? Did they lose these? For these are the wealth of Christians, to whom the wealthy apostle said, "Godliness with contentment is great gain. For we brought nothing into this world, and it is certain we can carry nothing out. And having food and raiment, let us be therewith content. But they that will be rich fall into temptation and a snare, and into many foolish and hurtful lusts, which drown men in destruction and perdition. For the love of money is the root of all evil; which, while some coveted after, they have erred from the faith, and pierced themselves through with many sorrows."

They, then, who lost their worldly all in the sack of Rome, if they owned their possessions as they had been taught by the apostle, who himself was poor without, but rich within,—that is to say, if they used the world as not using it,—could say in the words of Job, heavily tried, but not overcome: "Naked came I out of my mother's womb, and naked shall I return thither: the Lord gave, and the Lord hath taken away; as it pleased the Lord, so has it come to pass: blessed be the name of the Lord." Like a good servant, Job counted the will of his Lord his great possession, by obedience to which his soul was enriched; nor did it grieve him to lose, while yet living, those goods which he must shortly leave at his death. But as to those feebler spirits who, though they cannot be said to prefer earthly possessions to Christ, do yet cleave to them with a somewhat immoderate attachment, they have discovered by the pain of losing these things how much they were sinning in loving them. For their grief is of their own making; in the words of the apostle quoted above, "they have pierced themselves through with many sorrows." For it was well that they who had so long despised these verbal admonitions should receive the teaching of experience. For when the apostle says, "They that will be rich fall into temptation," and so on, what he blames in riches is not the possession of them, but the desire of them. For elsewhere he says, "Charge them that are rich in this world, that they be not high-minded, nor trust in uncertain riches, but in the living God, who giveth us richly all things to enjoy; that they do good, that they be rich in good works, ready to distribute, willing to communicate; laying up in store for themselves a good foundation against the time to come, that they may lay hold on eternal life." They who were making such a use of their property have been consoled for light losses by great gains, and have had more pleasure in those possessions which they have securely laid past, by freely giving them away, than grief in those which they entirely lost by an anxious and selfish hoarding of them. For nothing could perish on earth save what they would be ashamed to carry away from earth. Our Lord's injunction runs, "Lay not up for yourselves treasures upon earth, where moth and rust doth corrupt, and where thieves break through and steal; but lay up for yourselves treasures in heaven, where neither moth nor rust doth corrupt, and where thieves do not break through nor steal: for where your treasure is, there will your heart be also." And they who have listened to this injunction have proved in the time of tribulation how well they were advised in not despising this most trustworthy teacher, and most faithful and mighty guardian of their treasure. For if many were glad that their treasure was stored in places which the enemy chanced not to light upon, how much better founded was the joy of those who, by the counsel of their God, had fled with their treasure to a citadel which no enemy can possibly reach! Thus our Paulinus, bishop of Nola, who voluntarily abandoned vast wealth and became quite poor, though abundantly rich in holiness, when the barbarians sacked Nola, and took him prisoner, used silently to pray, as he afterwards told me, "O Lord, let me not be troubled for gold and silver, for where all my treasure is Thou knowest." For all his treasure was where he had been taught to hide and store it by Him who had also foretold that these calamities would happen in the world. Consequently those persons who obeyed their Lord when He warned them where and how to lay up treasure, did not lose even their earthly possessions in the invasion of the barbarians; while those who are now repenting that they did not obey Him have learnt the right use of earthly goods, if not by the wisdom which would have prevented their loss, at least by the experience which follows it.

But some good and Christian men have been put to the torture, that they might be forced to deliver up their goods to the enemy. They could indeed neither deliver nor lose that good which made themselves good. If, however, they preferred torture to the surrender of the mammon of iniquity, then I say they were not good men. Rather they should have been reminded that, if they suffered so severely for the sake of money, they should endure all torment, if need be, for Christ's sake; that they might be taught to love Him rather who enriches with eternal felicity all who suffer for Him, and not silver and gold, for which it was pitiable to suffer, whether they preserved it by telling a lie or lost it by telling the truth. For under these tortures no one lost Christ by confessing Him, no one preserved wealth save by denying its existence. So that possibly the torture which taught them that they should set their affections on a possession they could not lose, was more useful than those possessions which, without any useful fruit at all, disquieted and tormented their anxious owners. But then we are reminded that some were tortured who had no wealth to surrender, but who were not believed when they said so. These too, however, had perhaps some craving for wealth, and were not willingly poor with a holy resignation; and to such it had to be made plain, that not the actual possession alone, but also the desire of wealth, deserved such excruciating pains. And even if they were destitute of any hidden stores of gold and silver, because they were living in hopes of a better life,—I know not indeed if any such person was tortured on the supposition that he had wealth; but if so, then certainly in confessing, when put to the question, a holy poverty, he confessed Christ. And though it was scarcely to be expected that the barbarians should believe him, yet no confessor of a holy poverty could be tortured without receiving a heavenly reward.

Again, they say that the long famine laid many a Christian low. But this, too, the faithful turned to good uses by a pious endurance of it. For those whom famine killed outright it rescued from the ills of this life, as a kindly disease would have done; and those who were only hunger-bitten were taught to live more sparingly, and inured to longer fasts.

Chapter 15.—Of the Man Christ Jesus, the Mediator Between God and Men.

But if, as is much more probable and credible, it must needs be that all men, so long as they are mortal, are also miserable, we must seek an intermediate who is not only man, but also God, that, by the interposition of His blessed mortality, He may bring men out of their mortal misery to a blessed immortality. In this intermediate two things are requisite, that He become mortal, and that He do not continue mortal. He did become mortal, not rendering the divinity of the Word infirm, but assuming the infirmity of flesh. Neither did He continue mortal in the flesh, but raised it from the dead; for it is the very fruit of His mediation that those, for the sake of whose redemption He became the Mediator, should not abide eternally in

bodily death. Wherefore it became the Mediator between us and God to
have both a transient mortality and a permanent blessedness, that by that
which is transient He might be assimilated to mortals, and might translate
them from mortality to that which is permanent. Good angels, therefore,
cannot mediate between miserable mortals and blessed immortals, for they
themselves also are both blessed and immortal; but evil angels can mediate,
because they are immortal like the one party, miserable like the other. To
these is opposed the good Mediator, who, in opposition to their immortality and misery, has chosen to be mortal for a time, and has been able to
continue blessed in eternity. It is thus He has destroyed, by the humility of
His death and the benignity of His blessedness, those proud immortals and
hurtful wretches, and has prevented them from seducing to misery by their
boast of immortality those men whose hearts He has cleansed by faith, and
whom He has thus freed from their impure dominion.

Man, then, mortal and miserable, and far removed from the immortal and
the blessed, what medium shall he choose by which he may be united to
immortality and blessedness? The immortality of the demons, which might
have some charm for man, is miserable; the mortality of Christ, which
might offend man, exists no longer. In the one there is the fear of an eternal misery; in the other, death, which could not be eternal, can no longer be
feared, and blessedness, which is eternal, must be loved. For the immortal
and miserable mediator interposes himself to prevent us from passing to
a blessed immortality, because that which hinders such a passage, namely,
misery, continues in him; but the mortal and blessed Mediator interposed
Himself, in order that, having passed through mortality, He might of mortals make immortals (showing His power to do this in His own resurrection), and from being miserable to raise them to the blessed company from
the number of whom He had Himself never departed. There is, then, a
wicked mediator, who separates friends, and a good Mediator, who recon-
ciles enemies. And those who separate are numerous, because the multitude
of the blessed are blessed only by their participation in the one God; of
which participation the evil angels being deprived, they are wretched, and
interpose to hinder rather than to help to this blessedness, and by their very
number prevent us from reaching that one beatific good, to obtain which

we need not many but one Mediator, the uncreated Word of God, by whom all things were made, and in partaking of whom we are blessed. I do not say that He is Mediator because He is the Word, for as the Word He is supremely blessed and supremely immortal, and therefore far from miserable mortals; but He is Mediator as He is man, for by His humanity He shows us that, in order to obtain that blessed and beatific good, we need not seek other mediators to lead us through the successive steps of this attainment, but that the blessed and beatific God, having Himself become a partaker of our humanity, has afforded us ready access to the participation of His divinity. For in delivering us from our mortality and misery, He does not lead us to the immortal and blessed angels, so that we should become immortal and blessed by participating in their nature, but He leads us straight to that Trinity, by participating in which the angels themselves are blessed. Therefore, when He chose to be in the form of a servant, and lower than the angels, that He might be our Mediator, He remained higher than the angels, in the form of God,—Himself at once the way of life on earth and life itself in heaven.

Tim Kimberley teaches LIVE through these theologians in a lively, fun format for churches and organizations.

To book Tim to please contact us through CredoHouse.org

Additional Church History DVD curriculum, iPhone Apps and Books covering many eras and details of Theology and Church History are available through CredoHouse.org